W9-COX-828

SOVIET TRADE
WITH
EASTERN EUROPE
1945 - 1949

MARGARET DEWAR

ROYAL INSTITUTE
OF INTERNATIONAL AFFAIRS

Price 8s. 6d. net

SOVIET TRADE WITH EASTERN EUROPE
1945–1949

THE ROYAL INSTITUTE
OF INTERNATIONAL AFFAIRS
London: Chatham House, St James's Square, S.W.1
New York: 542 Fifth Avenue, New York 19

Toronto   Bombay
Melbourne   Wellington   Cape Town
OXFORD UNIVERSITY PRESS

SOVIET TRADE
WITH EASTERN EUROPE
1945—1949

by

MARGARET DEWAR

London & New York

ROYAL INSTITUTE
OF INTERNATIONAL AFFAIRS

The Royal Institute of International Affairs is an unofficial and non-political body, founded in 1920 to encourage and facilitate the scientific study of international questions. The Institute, as such, is precluded by the terms of its Royal Charter from expressing an opinion on any aspect of international affairs. Any opinions expressed in this publication are not, therefore, those of the Institute.

First published 1951

PRINTED IN GREAT BRITAIN
AT THE BROADWATER PRESS, WELWYN GARDEN CITY
HERTFORDSHIRE

HF
3626
D51
c.2

CONTENTS

N 136g 62

27 July 62 – Oxford Univ. Press – (Econ)

v

ACKNOWLEDGEMENTS

I SHOULD like to express my thanks to Mr G. Ionescu, Dr G. Kemény, Dr J. A. Kronsten, Mr Norman Kirby, Mr J. W. D. Peel, and the members of the Soviet Studies sub-Committee of the Royal Institute of International Affairs, who have helped me with their advice.

M. D.

December 1949

Chapter One

INTRODUCTION

BEFORE the Second World War the bulk of the foreign trade of the Central and South Eastern European States was directed westwards, chiefly towards Germany, Great Britain, and the United States. Trade within the area was relatively small—about 15 per cent of the total—while that with the USSR was negligible. Today the picture is changed. Germany has become an insignificant trade partner, whereas the USSR, although she has not replaced Germany, plays a dominant part in the economic life of the Central and South Eastern European countries and their foreign trade. Hitler's attempt at an integration of their economies into that of Germany—his vision of a *Grossdeutscher Wirtschaftsraum*—began a process of creating large economic areas. This process is continued by both the E.R.P. countries and the USSR with its satellites, though the methods used, both political and economic, are different. For the present, neither of these areas is economically self-sufficient, and on both sides efforts are made to increase trade between the East and the West, for trade in the period immediately after the war had come almost to a standstill.

The questions therefore arise: What have the Central and South Eastern European countries (briefly referred to here as Eastern European countries) to offer by way of export goods? How far are their export surpluses limited by inter-regional trade, and in particular, what are their commitments under agreements with the USSR? It is the second question with which this study is chiefly concerned.

During the Second World War the economies of the Eastern European countries were geared entirely to the needs of the German war machine. This resulted in a trend towards greater industrialization and, in such countries as Czechoslovakia, Poland, and Hungary, in a change in the structure of industry, stress being laid on the development of heavy industry. This fact alone would have meant a re-orientation of post-war foreign trade, unless they chose to re-convert their industries to pre-war structure. The collapse of Germany created an economic and political vacuum in the Eastern European area. In the circumstances it was almost inevitable that the USSR should move in. The entire area became a Soviet 'sphere of influence'. The countries concerned were in varying stages of economic dislocation, with industries and transport systems practically at a standstill, currencies enormously inflated, and agriculture severely hit by droughts in the years immediately following the war. All this made the resumption of foreign trade, particularly with the Western countries, very difficult. The USSR on the other hand, was near by with liberating, or occupying, troops, and at least some transport facilities. She relieved the desperate shortage of food by loans of grain, and concluded trade agreements for the supply of raw materials and other essential goods in exchange for whatever the Eastern countries had to offer. The total volume of trade was, admittedly, only a fraction of that of pre-war; yet within these limits, and excluding the special question of Unrra relief, the USSR in 1945–6 became the main supplier and customer of Eastern Europe. For the Soviet Union it was, of course, a matter of major concern to 'get in first', and the Eastern European countries had no alternative other than to comply. They had to choose between trade with the USSR on the terms offered, or no trade at all.

But post-war economic relations between the USSR and the Eastern European countries were not restricted to trade alone; they were much more complicated and far-reaching. Soviet economic policy towards these States was contradictory. Particularly in the immediate post-war period, the USSR sought to extract from Eastern Europe as much capital equipment and goods as possible. At the same time, Russia, in her own interest, was greatly concerned in helping these countries to rehabilitate their economy and to mould it according to the Soviet pattern. The first trend was more marked in the ex-enemy countries, Hungary and Roumania. Here, and to some extent in Bulgaria, economic relations were expressed through three channels. First, through reparations, claims for the maintenance of the occupation troops, and the taking over of German and Italian assets which meant the dismantling, removal of equipment, acquisition of plants, enterprises, and interests. Second, control over natural resources, key industries, and important public services through the establishments of jointly owned companies

2

and in some countries (Hungary, Germany, and probably others) of Soviet-owned enterprises, operating primarily in the interest of the USSR.

Third, there were the regular trade agreements. Czechoslovakia, Poland, and Yugoslavia, as allied countries, and Bulgaria (which occupied an in-between position, and was made to pay reparations only to Yugoslavia and Greece, but not to the USSR) were treated with more regard than Hungary and Roumania, though Poland (and probably Bulgaria) suffered dismantling and removal of ex-enemy goods, particularly in the former German territories. Economic relations with these countries are regulated by agreements on economic co-operation, exchange of goods, industrial credits, and even gold loans. The Soviet press continually asserts that these agreements are concluded as between equal sovereign States. There seems little doubt however that the terms of the agreements are applied with greater strictness to the satellite countries than to the USSR herself.

The dominating position of the USSR in the trade of Eastern Europe, notably in Czechoslovakia, Poland, and Hungary, was of a temporary nature, as is borne out by later development. It arose out of war conditions and the post-war situation: Eastern Europe needed first and foremost food and raw materials (which the Soviet Union, probably chiefly for political reasons, was anxious and able to supply) and it had little to offer that was of interest to the West. During this phase the USSR succeeded in firmly establishing her economic hold over those countries.

By the beginning or middle of 1947 a new economic pattern started to emerge: the post-war rehabilitation period was more or less over and there began a period of further development of the national economies, which proceeded very much on Soviet lines. In all Eastern European countries national economic plans were adopted, aiming at considerable expansion of industry and a mechanization of agriculture. These determine the foreign trade needs and potentialities.

Whatever the final aim of the Soviet Union may be in regard to the creation of a self-sufficient economic area in the East with the greatest possible independence from the West, the needs of the Eastern European countries for capital goods and raw materials, on which the fulfilment of their plans depends, are greater than the USSR's capacity to satisfy them. Consequently they have to turn to the West. This is, at the present stage, by no means discouraged by the USSR, especially as the Eastern European countries often appear to act as buyers for Russia. On the contrary, the desire for increased trade with the West is emphasized, and no opportunity is neglected to 'deplore' any decline or unsatisfactory development of trade with Western countries. Any deterioration in trade relations is invariably attributed to 'restrictions' imposed on trade with the East 'for political reasons'; in the first instance by the United States, but also other countries of the West. Far too little recognition, at any rate in the Eastern press, is given to the fact that successful trading, though restricted by certain considerations of national security and the settlement of compensation claims of Western interests, depends equally on purely commercial considerations (i.e. whether the goods offered by the East have a practical use-value for the West). Their range is indeed limited and they are often available only conditionally, for example, in exchange for steel or other scarce materials, which the West is not willing or able to supply. Other obstacles are delivery and terms offered or asked for. Yet in principle trade with the West is encouraged by the Soviet and the Eastern European Governments and has, in fact, greatly increased since 1945–6.[1] It is, obviously, an expedient confined to goods indispensable for the execution of the plans. But there are, at any rate at present, few signs of creating an economically self-sufficient area in the East, nor does there seem much likelihood that this can be done in the near future.[2]

A new phase in the economic relations in Eastern Europe was introduced by the formation in January 1949 of the Council of Mutual Economic Assistance, the aims of which are stated

[1] For details see 'The Commodity Composition of Trade between Eastern and Western Europe in 1948' in *The Economic Bulletin for Europe*, second quarter, vol. 1, no. 2. Economic Commission for Europe (Geneva 1949).

[2] Mr Hilary Minc, Polish Minister of Trade and Industry and Deputy Chairman of the Council of Ministers, says: 'As for the foreign trade and economic relations with capitalist countries, the task of planning in the People's Democracies is to secure such an organization of these relations as will increase to the maximum the economic power of the given country, making it more independent of the capitalist economy, and creating conditions for the speediest advance towards Socialism. Consequently, in planning foreign trade between the People's Democracies and capitalist countries it is not the aim of the former to secure the broadest development of these relations, irrespective of their content and the results, but to establish relations which will facilitate the strengthening of the given country in its position as a Socialist State.' *For a Lasting Peace, for a People's Democracy* (Bucharest, 18 November 1949).

to be 'broader economic co-operation among the countries of the People's Democracy and the USSR'.[1] Its task is 'the exchange of experience in the economic field, the rendering of technical assistance to one another, and the rendering of mutual assistance in regard to raw materials, food-stuffs, machinery, equipment, etc.' Czechoslovakia, Bulgaria, Hungary, Poland, Roumania, and the USSR participated in the opening conference. Yugoslavia was not invited, but the Conference resolution stated that 'the Council shall be an open organization, which may be joined by other countries of Europe that share the principles of the Council. . .' In February 1949 Albania became a member. The positive functions of the Council as a co-ordinating body would appear to be a sufficient explanation for its setting up. A political propaganda note was, however, added by the declaration of the Conference that 'the Governments of the United States, Britain, and of certain other countries of Western Europe have been, as a matter of fact, boycotting trade relations with the countries of the People's Democracy and with the USSR', allegedly because the latter countries did not 'submit to the Marshall Plan dictate'.

It remains to be seen whether the Council for Mutual Economic Assistance will in time become an over-all directing body, not only for trade, but for planning the production of the entire Eastern area as well. In spite of unconfirmed reports of a twenty years' treaty concluded in Moscow at a secret meeting in May 1949, and the creation of a 100 million rouble fund to balance payments (in the first place to Czechoslovakia), there is not sufficient evidence to support such an assumption. The brief communiqué on the first public meeting of the Council since its foundation, held in Sofia at the end of August 1949, does not disclose anything about its activities.[2] Mr Minc, the most outstanding and efficient organizer in the economic field in the East European countries, whose pronouncements can be considered authoritative, expressed the view[3] (admitted-

[1] *Soviet Monitor* (25 January 1949).   [2] *Pravda* (29 August 1949)
[3] 'The all round development of foreign trade and of the general economic relations between the People's Democracies and the Soviet Union accelerates the growth of the productive forces and the victory of Socialism, strengthens planning in the People's Democracies and makes it possible to extend the co-ordination in planning between several countries. The Council of Mutual Economic Aid is the organizational form which accelerates the accumulation of experience and crystallization of these essentially new economic relations'. *For a Lasting Peace, for a People's Democracy* (18 November 1949).

ly in a somewhat vague and cryptic way) that the Council will encourage the co-ordination of the plans between the People's Democracies and the USSR, but so far no concrete evidence of this has come to light.

The Council's initial step was, as far as is known, probably the first tri-lateral barter contracts between Russia–Poland– Finland, and Russia–Czechoslovakia–Finland (the latter is not a member of the Council). Hitherto trade agreements both with the USSR and inter-regionally were strictly bi-lateral. Two post-war phases can be distinguished: at first they were short-term agreements, mostly for one year. With the gradual stabilization of the economic trends in the East, and the adoption of the Marshall Plan in the West, the tendency since the middle of 1947 has, however, gravitated towards treaties with a longer run, usually for five years. A number of important agreements (on trade, credits, and reparation reductions) was concluded in the summer of 1947; they were obviously meant as a compensation for the non-participation of the Eastern countries in the Marshall Plan. The Eastern European countries clearly had no choice and they consoled themselves by stressing the advantages of trade with the USSR, which, they said, was restricted to essential goods only, whereas under the Marshall Plan they would have had to accept non-essential goods as well.

The trade treaties between the Soviet Union and the Eastern European countries are as a rule barter agreements with a reciprocal most-favoured-nation clause in regard to customs duties, taxes and fees, navigation and transit. Provision is usually made for the USSR to have trade delegations in the other contracting countries. In some, if not in all countries, joint Chambers of Commerce have been established. Under the trade treaties in the early stages after the war so-called 'hire-work' contracts were much favoured: the USSR supplied the raw material, mainly cotton, and part of the finished product was then imported into the Soviet Union. Such procedure helped to pay for the raw cotton received, at the same time providing employment to the workers. This system now seems to have been practically discontinued.

The agreements are usually concluded for a total value of goods, which up to recently was always expressed in dollars (these were, obviously, used only as a unit of account without any exchanges of currency taking place). Since 1949, however, all agreements are expressed in roubles.

The range of goods to be exchanged under a trade agreement is laid down in 'special protocols' by the negotiating Government delegations on general lines, to be specified later, together with delivery terms, within the limits of the agreed quota. In some instances provision is made for an exchange of goods over and above the fixed quota. All payments are made to, and by, the respective State or National Banks from non-interest-bearing dollar accounts especially opened for that purpose. These accounts are supposed to balance. Provision is, however, made in the agreements for the settlement of any adverse balances that may have arisen either by means of supplementary deliveries of goods or by gold or freely convertible currency at an agreed rate of exchange.

With regard to prices asked for, and paid, by the Soviet Union, there is much vagueness and doubt. In the trade agreements up to 1949 they were usually stated to be based on world market prices expressed in U.S. dollars. This, however, is by no means favourable to all Eastern European countries where production costs are, as for example in Hungary, much above world market prices. Moreover, for heavy engineering and capital goods no such prices exist and they are arrived at individually by agreement between two contracting Powers. In any case such a clause in agreements between the USSR and Eastern Europe appears rather meaningless, since trade is conducted almost exclusively on the basis of barter and since different rates of conversion are applied according to the nature of the goods and their origin and destination. It is, in fact, known that the USSR has worked out an entire system of different conversion rates.[1] No authentic information could be obtained on prices, but it does seem that prices charged by the USSR tend to be high and those offered low, especially when it is a question of buying goods for re-export (Roumanian grain, Bulgarian tobacco, Yugoslav metals, Polish coke) on which the USSR no doubt makes considerable profits.

It must also be remembered that the fixing of prices in the

---

[1] For conversion rates for Polish coal supplied to Russia, see *The East European Economy in Relation to the European Recovery Programme*, Preliminary Report Twenty of the House Select Committee on Foreign Aid, pursuant to H. Res. 296. (U.S.A. 7 March 1948) pp. 23–6, 33. (This Report will henceforth be referred to as the *Herter Report*).

Eastern countries with their nationalized industry and virtual trade monopoly is often a question of policy, irrespective of actual production costs. This was the case with the USSR during the first five-year plans, and is now apparently being repeated in the satellite countries.[1] In negotiations between the Eastern European countries and the USSR, the former are *a priori* in a weaker position, since prices are negotiated after the quotas have been fixed and the delegations are already committed to deliveries. This does not mean that they submit without any attempts at better terms, as shown by the example of the Bulgarian Vice-Premier Traicho Kostov, tried and sentenced to death in December 1949.[2] On the whole, however, the trade delegations from the Eastern European countries are under pressure; the initiative lies entirely with the Soviet representatives who prepare the agenda and the draft protocols, and who expect that Soviet tenders and offers will be accepted in preference to any others. Soviet requirements are such that they seem to take most of the goods offered to them, though they are not always satisfied with the quality. The quality of their own goods is no doubt mostly very poor, if one may judge from the frequent complaints in Soviet newspapers about the shoddiness of consumer goods. Having no competition to meet in the satellite countries, it is unlikely that the USSR will deliver goods greatly superior to those sold at home. It is equally impossible to obtain reliable information regarding the implementation of the trade agreements. It is probably true, as reported by individuals, that USSR deliveries of grain and raw materials (particularly in the early post-war years) arrived

---

[1] Czechoslovakia is selling Tudor automobiles in her own country for 250,000 Kčs; to Poland for 98,000 Kčs (approximate cost price); to the Netherlands and Pakistan at 38,000 Kčs, and to other countries at prices somewhere between those of the Dutch and the Polish.

[2] The charges made against Traicho Kostov were, *inter alia*, that while conducting trade talks and giving economic information to Soviet representatives he had shown 'an insincere and unfriendly policy towards the Soviet Union'. (Resolution of the CC of the Bulgarian Communist Party, published in *Rabotnichesko Delo*, 5 April 1949). At the trial Kostov was accused of imperilling the conclusion of trade deals when negotiating in Moscow by arguing on every point: the exchange rate of the rouble; the question of German assets; the prices of Bulgarian tobacco and Soviet goods and the suggested devaluation of Bulgarian credits after the devaluation of the Soviet rouble (*The Times*, 9 December 1949). Another telling example of Soviet or Communist Party pressure is the exclusion from the Party of a director of Metalimport for 'his anti-Soviet disposition' expressed in a telegram to the Bulgarian Ambassador in Moscow 'with anti-Soviet contents' (obviously referring to some trade terms). The Chief Director of Metalimport was severely reprimanded for lack of vigilance (*Rabotnichesko Delo*, 12 November 1949).

promptly, but that delays occurred in the delivery of machines and equipment, and that the USSR is, on the whole, unable to satisfy the needs of the Eastern European countries for capital goods. It is probably also correct to say that the satellite countries endeavour to be more punctual and meticulous in carrying out the terms of the agreements than the USSR.

The methods and channels of foreign trade in the Eastern European countries are more or less identical. A virtual trade monopoly exists in all of them. Foreign trade is controlled by the State through the Ministries of Trade and Commerce and is operated by State monopoly companies for each branch of industry in conformity with the national economic plan.[1] Even when allowances are made for the economic structure of the People's Democracies, still somewhat different from that of the present-day USSR (but comparable perhaps to the so-called N.E.P. period with its mixed economy),[2] the methods and organization of foreign trade are very much on Soviet lines.

The same is becoming equally evident in regard to the publication of statistics. Roumania and Yugoslavia do not seem to publish any at all. Bulgaria, Czechoslovakia, Hungary, and Poland, until the middle or end of 1948, published fairly comprehensive trade figures. They still issue various statistical bulletins, but for practical purposes these have become almost useless—at any rate so far as trade is concerned—since, one by one, these countries have discontinued to give analyses by countries and values. They confine themselves to total figures of trade turnover[3] and to analyses by commodities only. The USSR herself, as is known, has not published comprehensive statistics since the middle of the nineteen-thirties. Figures given in Soviet articles dealing with trade of the Eastern European countries (chiefly in *Vneshnaya Torgovlya*,[4] published in Moscow) are mostly incomplete and often in non-comparable percentages. The USSR is nearly always omitted or referred to in a general

---

[1] In the USSR a foreign trade monopoly has existed since 1918. For a detailed description of its functioning, with particular reference to trade with Great Britain, see *Soviet Foreign Trade* by Alexander Baykov (New Jersey, Princeton University Press, 1946).

[2] The period from 1921–8 when private and socialized enterprises and trade co-existed.

[3] Bulgaria has passed a law on State secrets, defined to include all actual production and trade figures. This was obviously done under the influence of the USSR decree on State secrets of 9 June 1947.

[4] Journal of the Ministry of Foreign Trade of the USSR.

way only, without any figures being quoted. For the purpose of this study it has therefore been necessary to rely, in addition to original sources such as are available, to a large extent on brief notes in the *Soviet News* and the *Soviet Monitor*. These sources were supplemented by the Western daily press, by Unrra and ECE reports, as well as by private information which has been considered sufficiently reliable and informative.

Consequently, the material here collected is necessarily incomplete. Even so, it is hoped that the information compiled will help to give a picture of economic and trade relations in Eastern Europe and enable conclusions to be drawn about the scope left for trade with the West.

The development of post-war trade between the USSR and Eastern Europe is treated separately for each country in the following order: first the 'allied' countries: Czechoslovakia and Poland; Bulgaria, which occupies an intermediate position; then the ex-enemy countries Hungary and Roumania. The study concludes with Yugoslavia, which today is in a special category, but which, during most of the period under discussion, was still a member of the Eastern economic sphere. Relations with Czechoslovakia have been given at somewhat greater length, not only because the material available was more abundant, but also because it was felt that the attitude of Czechoslovakia towards trade and close economic relations with the USSR, as expressed by its Government even before the February 1948 coup, was probably characteristic of some of the other Eastern European countries as well, in view of their changed economic and social post-war structure. It is realized, however, that such countries as Hungary and Roumania, at any rate, had little choice. Quotations given from official statements in the various sections serve the purpose of explaining the economic and political reasons for the change in the direction of trade as seen by these countries themselves. No attempt has been made to give a critical appraisal of these statements and of the political opinions expressed, or even of the trade trends as part of the general economic development of the Eastern European countries.

The purpose of this study was simply to collect such data as are available on the nature and extent of the exchange of goods between Eastern Europe and the USSR (not including the Eastern zone of Germany, Finland). The very brief outline in each section of the respective country's position during the war, its pre-war trade, and post-war economic trends are given merely as a background. A full analysis of future trends, and in particular an appraisal of trade possibilities with the West, could be given only on the basis of a study of the entire post-war economic development in the East.

Chapter Two

CZECHOSLOVAKIA

In March 1939 Czechoslovakia was invaded by Hitler. Bohemia and Moravia, the highly industrialized parts of the country, were annexed and subsequently administered as a 'protectorate'; Slovakia was set up as an independent puppet State, and Sub-Carpathian Ruthenia occupied by Hungary.

The Czechoslovak Government fled first to France, then to London, and in November 1939 set up a Czechoslovak National Committee, which in July 1940 constituted itself as the Provisional Government, and in July 1941—with the consent and recognition of the Allies—as the Government of the ČSR. It immediately declared its country to be at war with all nations fighting the Allies, and with Germany, in particular, since March 1939.

The first agreement on mutual aid and support in the war against Germany between the Governments of Czechoslovakia and the USSR was signed in July 1941; it included the constitution on Soviet territory of Czechoslovak military units. A Treaty of Friendship, Mutual Assistance, and Post-war Collaboration followed in December 1943.[1] It contained a clause (Article 4) that the High Contracting Powers 'agree to develop to the widest possible degree their economic relations and to render each other every possible economic assistance after the war'.

Other agreements (on military and monetary matters) followed in 1944 and the first post-war trade agreement with the USSR was concluded in September 1945.

CHANGES IN ECONOMY DURING THE WAR

During the Second World War Czechoslovakia's industry suffered relatively little damage. It underwent, however, considerable changes under the German occupation since it was made to serve primarily the needs of the German war machine. Her heavy industry was greatly expanded, while the capacity of her light and consumer goods industry was much reduced.

[1] *Vneshnaya Torgovlya*, no. 1 (1944) pp. 10 ff.

After the war Czechoslovakia had the choice of either returning to her pre-war production of predominantly semi-processed and manufactured goods, or of continuing along the road chosen for her by the Nazis—the expansion of her heavy industries at the expense of light and consumer goods industries. In the latter case she would have to re-orientate her foreign trade and look for new markets and new sources of raw materials. In view of Germany's economic collapse Czechoslovakia stood a good chance of taking her place in the market for heavy industry goods. This was expressed by the late President Beneš in a speech on 20 July 1946 in Moravska-Ostrava: 'The adjustment of production in Germany will entail considerable reconstruction of our economy. In particular, German armament and heavy industrial production will be reduced and some peace-time production increased. As a result of this change we may be able to supply markets in Eastern and South Eastern Europe, as well as overseas.'[1]

An Unrra report[2] came to similar conclusions: 'The social and economic reforms in post-war Europe seemed to offer another opportunity for Czechoslovakian trade. In most countries, and in particular in Eastern Europe, plans were being made for widespread industrialization. These plans would produce a new and large demand for the products of heavy industry. Moreover, industrialization, coupled with the social demands of new classes of population, seemed to assure an expansion in the European market for consumer goods.'

Taking into further consideration the difficulties of obtaining foreign credits, of trading with the dollar and sterling areas, as well as the general political set-up in Europe after the war, it is perhaps not surprising that Czechoslovakia turned towards the East, redirecting there a substantial part of her foreign trade, and organizing and planning her economy accordingly. The necessity for this has been repeatedly stressed by her Government officials, both before and after the February 1948 coup. Yet it is precisely in the interest of the successful carrying out of her economic plans that Czechoslovakia has shown no desire to cease trade with the West. Indeed, various Government statements (since February 1948, no doubt Soviet-inspired and in accord with the latter's policy) point to the contrary.

---

[1] Unrra, OAP, no. 16, *Industrial Rehabilitation in Czechoslovakia* (1947) p. 16.
[2] ibid. no. 21, *The Foreign Trade of Czechoslovakia* (1947) p. 7.

Mr Klement Gottwald, then Prime Minister, declared, for example, to the Constituent National Assembly on 8 July 1946:

Czechoslovakia herself does not possess sufficient quantities of raw materials, therefore the realization of the two-year plan will, to a large extent, depend on foreign trade. . . Our foreign trade must develop on such lines as to secure permanent markets for our products and permanent sources of supply of raw materials, which will be independent of economic crises. Therefore, in the first place it is necessary to develop extensively and to strengthen the economic links with the Soviet Union, the other Slav States and the Central and South Eastern European countries. At the same time, we shall systematically develop our economic relations with the United States, Great Britain, France, and other countries.[1]

The same case was argued in 1948 by the present Czechoslovak Foreign Trade Minister, Dr Antonin Gregor, in an interview reported in the *Central European Trade Review*.[2] 'By the end of 1953, [end of the five-year economic plan] Czechoslovakia's neighbours will account for 45 per cent of her foreign trade.' The greater part, he emphasized, will still be with the rest of the world. Dr V. Clementis in a speech at the Economic Committee of the United Nations also stressed that increased trade with Eastern Europe did not mean a cutting down of trade with the West. On the contrary, he pointed out that Czechoslovak exports to the Marshall Plan countries compared favourably with pre-war trade and he expressed the conviction that 'political realities' ought not to be 'any obstacle to economic co-operation'.[3]

POST-WAR INDUSTRIAL DEVELOPMENT

Czechoslovakia was the first of the countries in the Soviet orbit to commence (24 October 1945) with the nationalization of her basic industry and large-scale enterprises. Further laws followed and by mid-1948 nationalization of all industry was practically complete. A land redistribution also took place, an agrarian reform having been carried out by the newly-established Republic after the First World War. In October 1946 a two-year economic plan was adopted for 1947 and 1948. It aimed at a general increase in the standard of living and a wider

---

[1] *Vneshnaya Torgovlya*, no. 6 (1947) p. 9.　　[2] No. 4 (1948) p. 56.
[3] *Czechoslovak Economic Bulletin*, Czechoslovak Ministry of Foreign Trade, no. 155 (1948) pp. 2, 3.

distribution of industry over the country. (One-third of the capital investment, for example, was allocated to Slovakia.) Production, with emphasis on heavy industry, was to increase 10 per cent over the pre-war level. Much attention was to be paid to higher technical efficiency and to increased exports. The total investment was planned at $1,390,000,000, two-sevenths of which were to go to industry; 239,000 new workers were to be drawn into industry. Increased output was planned for agricultural machinery, and production of synthetic fuel was to be taken up for the first time. With regard to consumer industries, it was intended to bring production of textiles and shoes up to the level that would cover pre-war consumption and provide a surplus for the exports necessary for the payment of raw materials.[1]

A more comprehensive five-year plan, covering the years 1949 to 1953, was adopted by the Czechoslovak Government in October 1948. It envisages a 57 per cent overall increase in industrial production over 1948 and continues to stress the further development of heavy industry to which 72 per cent of all industrial capital investments are allocated. In particular the following increases in the gross value of production compared with 1948 are planned: engineering 93 per cent; iron and steel 49 per cent; mining 35 per cent; power 52 per cent. The production of other manufactured goods will, relatively speaking, decrease. For the total agricultural production an increase of 37 per cent over the reduced production plan for 1948 is foreseen with particular emphasis on livestock (in 1953 to constitute 48 per cent of total agriculture, instead of 35 per cent as in 1948). An important aspect of the plan is increased foreign trade (approximately 40 per cent over 1948) and long-term economic agreements, 'in particular with the countries with planned economies'.[2]

One such long-term agreement, for a period of five years, was concluded with Poland in July 1947, which was to operate under a joint Council for Czechoslovak-Polish Economic Co-operation. It was suggested at that time by press correspondents that the expanding industries of those two countries together might create a 'second Ruhr in the East'.[3] It is difficult

---

[1] Unrra, OAP, no. 16, op. cit. p. 18.

[2] *The First Czechoslovak Economic Five-Year Plan*, Czechoslovak Ministry of Information and Public Culture (2nd ed., February 1949, Prague).

[3] *The Times* (5 August 1947); *Czechoslovak Economic Bulletin*, no. 89 (1949) p. 3.

to assess how far this will become a reality; the potentialities are perhaps there, even taking into consideration that the economies of the two countries are not entirely complementary. A more serious obstacle to such an enterprise is probably the Soviet Government's distrust for large economic (and potentially political) conglomerations not run by themselves. According to private information given by an ex-Government official of one of these countries, the agreement when concluded did not at all meet with the wholehearted approval of the Soviet Government. Be that as it may, it does appear that economic co-operation between Poland and Czechoslovakia has so far not gone much beyond appointing a number of committees and of agreeing on one power plant project. Official reports from the respective countries do not seem to go beyond general statements on an increased volume of trade and on various large-scale industrial projects agreed upon between the two Governments.[1]

RESUMPTION OF TRADE

In contrast to most Central and South Eastern European States, Czechoslovakia before 1939 was an advanced industrial country. Having inherited the industrial core of the old Austro-Hungarian Empire, and only a small part of its population, Czechoslovakia, from her inception, became vitally dependent on foreign markets for her industrial and agricultural surplus goods, and for the raw materials required for her industries. In 1937, for example, raw materials amounted to 58 per cent of her total imports, and consisted chiefly of cotton, wool, iron ore, other metals, chemicals, hides; 72 per cent of her exports consisted of textiles, iron and steel products, manufactured goods such as glass, ceramics, shoes, gloves, and agricultural products, mainly sugar, malt, and hops.[2]

The foreign trade of Czechoslovakia was widely distributed over the world. Germany was the most important partner, but never rose to the dominant position she occupied in the trade of other Eastern European countries. In 1937 Germany supplied about 17 per cent of Czechoslovakia's total imports and pur-

---

[1] In August 1949 agreements were negotiated for the construction of a Czech zone in the Port of Stettin, for construction and navigation work on the river Oder, as well as several tariff agreements. *Czechoslovak Economic Bulletin*, no. 181 (1949) p. 4.

[2] W. Diamond, *Czechoslovakia between East and West* (London, Stevens, 1947) p. 126.

chased about 15 per cent of her exports. Next came the United
States with 8·7 and 9·3 per cent and the United Kingdom
with 6·3 and 8·7 per cent respectively. The Soviet Union's
share was 1·1 and 0·8 per cent, that of Eastern Europe 12·5
and 14·9 per cent respectively.[1]

Immediately after the end of the war production in Czechoslovakia fell to its lowest point. A number of industrial enterprises had been severely damaged in the last stages of the war,
stocks of raw materials were exhausted, while the transport
system came almost to a standstill. Industry suffered from a
shortage of skilled workers, the position being aggravated by the
expulsion of the Sudeten Germans; productivity in general
declined. All this made the resumption of foreign trade a
difficult task. However, the Czechoslovak Government, largely
with the help of Unrra, succeeded in getting the country's
economy on its feet and by the end of 1945 it had concluded
trade agreements with twelve countries and economic treaties
with Great Britain and Canada. The total foreign trade in
that year was obviously still very small. It amounted from May
to December to 407·6 million Kčs (crowns) on the export, and
to 604,0 million Kčs on the import side, i.e. its value amounted
to about 3·9 and 5·5 per cent respectively of the totals for
export and import in 1937. Taking into consideration the considerable increase in prices the actual volume of trade was
smaller still.[2]

The chief commercial supplier in 1945 was the USSR,
accounting for 32·7 per cent of Czechoslovakia's total imports;
the largest customer was Switzerland with 32·5 per cent; the
USSR in that year purchased 13 per cent of Czechoslovakian
exports.

In 1946 the USSR was Czechoslovakia's second best customer, taking 11·9 per cent of her total exports of Kčs 14,345
million, the first place being occupied by Switzerland (14·7
per cent). Third on the list with 9·9 per cent were the Eastern
European countries (Hungary, Yugoslavia, Bulgaria, Roumania, and Poland). On the import side these countries combined occupied the first place, accounting for 18·1 per cent of
Czechoslovakia's total imports of Kčs 10,239 millions; the
USSR was third with 9·6 per cent, following Switzerland with

[1] Unrra, OAP, no. 21, *The Foreign Trade of Czechoslovakia* (1947) p. 5.
[2] ibid. p. 9.

10·6 per cent. The share of the United Kingdom and the United States was 2·9 and 7·6 per cent respectively on the export side, and 8·9 and 8·3 per cent on the import side.

The subsequent development of Czechoslovakia's trade with the East is shown in the following table. (Figures with the U.K. and the U.S.A. are given for comparison).[1]

	EXPORTS		IMPORTS	
	1947	*1948*	*1947*	*1948*
		TOTAL IN 000 KČS		
	28,608,900	37,648,290	28,635,100	37,716,244
		PERCENTAGE OF TOTAL		
U.S.S.R.	5·1	16·0	6·2	15·6
Poland	1·7	7·0	2·4	5·4
Yugoslavia	6·2	6·9	4·7	6·3
Bulgaria ⎫				
Hungary ⎬	6·4	8·2	6·0	8·3
Roumania ⎭				
U.K.	6·4	3·6	11·7	10·1
U.S.A.	4·4	3·1	10·2	4·8

In 1947 Czechoslovakia's chief trade was with the free currency areas (Switzerland, Sweden, and the Netherlands) which accounted for over one-fourth of her exports and just over a fifth of her imports. The Soviet Union occupied the seventh place only, her imports from Czechoslovakia having decreased from 11·9 to 5·1 per cent, due presumably to the long delivery times for the heavy industry goods, and her exports to Czechoslovakia having fallen from 9·6 to 6·2 per cent. Exports from the other Eastern European countries had also decreased from 18·1 to 13·1 per cent; but their imports from Czechoslovakia had, on the other hand, risen from 9·9 to 14·3 per cent.

In 1948, however, we again see an increase in the trade with the USSR which, with 16 per cent of Czechoslovakia's total exports and 15·6 of her imports, occupied the leading place. The share of Eastern Europe (excluding the USSR) rose in 1948 to 22·1 per cent of total Czechoslovak exports and 20 per cent of her total imports. Nevertheless, trade with all other countries remained predominant, amounting to 61·9 and 64·5 per cent respectively.

For 1949 no analyses by countries are available, the *Czechoslovak Economic Bulletin* having discontinued its practice of publishing fairly detailed trade figures. It is simply stated that the foreign trade turnover for the first half of 1949 amounted to 40,344 million Kčs which is roughly half of the 1948 total.

[1] Table based on *Czechoslovak Economic Bulletin*, no. 116 (1948) pp. 4, 10; no. 166 (1949) pp. 10, 11.

Structural changes in Czechoslovakia's foreign trade, in conformity with changes in her economy, are given in an article in *Obzor Narodohospodarsky*.[1] The export of machinery has risen from 8·8 per cent of the total in 1937 to 20·3 per cent in 1948 (January to October); the share of textiles and clothing has fallen from 25·1 to 15·7 per cent.

ORGANIZATION OF FOREIGN TRADE

The changes in Czechoslovakia's economic system have also required changes in the organization of her foreign trade, which reached their climax after the February coup of 1948, in the nationalization of the entire foreign trade. Modifying an earlier procedure, the Government, in the second half of 1948, decreed the separation of export and import activities from production in all branches of industry (with the exception of metal-working, rubber, and leather), and the setting-up of twenty-one monopoly trade companies which buy goods within the country for Czechoslovak crowns, and sell them abroad for foreign currency, and vice-versa.[2]

As to trade with the USSR, a Czechoslovak-Soviet Chamber of Commerce, with its seat in Prague, was founded early in 1947. At the session of the organizing committee in Moscow in March 1947 seventeen Soviet import and export organizations and a large number of industrial, commercial, and transport firms from the Czech side were nominated as members. This joint Chamber of Commerce is also empowered to settle any dispute on trade matters that may arise.[3]

POST-WAR TRADE WITH THE USSR

As already mentioned, the first post-war trade agreement with the USSR was concluded on 24 September 1945. The USSR was to supply Czechoslovakia with minerals, wool, cotton, petrol, and 250,000 tons of German coal. The USSR was to receive machines, industrial equipment, and other manufactured goods. It seems that details of this agreement were not laid down until March 1946 when a 'special protocol' was signed in Prague formulating the basis for the assessment of

[1] Quoted by *Czechoslovak Economic Bulletin*, no. 174 (1949) p. 17.
[2] ibid. no. 140 (1948) p. 4; *Vneshnaya Torgovlya*, no. 3 (1949) p. 4. For details on structure, terms of reference, etc. of the joint stock companies see *Vneshnaya Torgovlya*, no. 4 (1949) p. 31.
[3] *Czechoslovak Economic Bulletin*, nos. 72, 73 (1947) pp. 9, 11.

prices for mutual deliveries of goods arising from the Czecho-slovak-Soviet Trade Convention of 1945. This protocol fixed the final quota for imports from the USSR at about 1 milliard Kčs; the value of exports was slightly less. Prices were to be fixed at the level of current world market prices or, alternative-ly, the competitive prices of foreign tenders. Import and export goods were both to be priced on the same basis.[1] Under this agreement Czechoslovakia had received from the USSR up to March 1946, 80 per cent of the raw materials to be delivered. This constituted about 60 per cent of Czechoslovakia's total imports of raw materials. The Czechoslovak textile industry received 20 per cent of her wool and 60 per cent of her cotton requirements from the USSR (part of which was, in a manu-factured state, re-exported to that country). All linen and flax was of Soviet origin, and about 70 to 80 per cent of all imported metals; in particular zinc and nickel supplies came exclusively from the USSR. The petroleum products delivered were largely reparation payments to the USSR from Hungary, Austria, and Roumania. Similarly, four trainloads of buna from the Russian zone of Germany were sent to Czechoslovakia to be manu-factured into such articles as boots, rubber soles and heels, tyres, and technical goods, partly to meet the needs of the Russian Army.[2]

Czechoslovakia, on the other hand, had, up to March 1946, delivered only 40 per cent of the goods contracted for since these required a longer time for delivery, especially in those cases where their manufacture depended on the supply of Soviet raw materials.[3]

A new Czechoslovak-Soviet trade agreement was signed in Moscow on 12 April 1946. The chief items to be exchanged were again ores, metals, textile raw materials, industrial salt and potash, mineral oils, synthetic rubber, and animal products. The USSR was to supply some of these products from repara-tions received by her from Germany, Hungary, and Roumania. The principal exports from Czechoslovakia to the USSR were to be rolled iron and steel products, sheet glass, paper, textiles, leather goods, tyres, carborundum products, sugar, and hops.[4]

---

[1] ibid. no. 22 (1946) p. 3.   [2] ibid. nos. 21, 22, 23 (1946), pp. 4, 4, 8.
[3] Interview by *Tägliche Rundschau* (7 June 1946) with Minister of Industry, Bohumil Lausmann.
[4] Supplement to *Czechoslovak Economic Bulletin*, no. 89 (1947) p. 4.

The exchange of goods under this agreement was to be carried out under a series of special protocols negotiated successively by the appropriate authorities of both Governments. Each protocol was to set out for a short period the total volume and the types of goods to be exchanged. As explained by Dr Ripka,[1] Minister of Foreign Trade up to February 1948, both sides were to make a list of the goods in which they were chiefly interested, which would act as a general indicator for future deals. Deals may, however, be made in any goods not mentioned in the lists. Individual deliveries would be agreed upon on the basis of negotiations between the commercial organizations of both countries, and would be carried out under the supervision of State plenipotentiaries who would see to it that the terms agreed upon were properly carried out as regards quantity, quality, price, and terms of delivery, as agreed upon between the partners to the deal.

Prices were again said to be based on those of the world market, but nothing was made known as to the exchange rates to be applied. Payments arising from the exchange of goods under this agreement were to be mutually settled by one or the other of two parallel systems: Goods named in the special protocols on mutual deliveries were to be paid for under a clearing system for which purpose the National Bank of Czechoslovakia and the State Bank of the USSR were to open mutual non-interest bearing accounts in Czechoslovak crowns. From these accounts both banks would immediately pay debts due to exporters against documents presented without regard to the state of their cash accounts. It was important, however, that the values of the goods tendered by both sides under the terms of the protocols should always be approximately equivalent in order to avoid the accumulation of clearing balances. Any deliveries outside the protocol schedules, where complete freedom was allowed as regards quantity and value of the goods, would be paid for in free foreign exchange. Dr Ripka, in giving these explanations, added that the agreement on payments was thus very elastic, combining the advantages of a clearing system with those of purchases by free foreign exchange.[2] Upon his return from Moscow, he expressed himself favourably on the new trade agreement which, he considered, contrary to that of

[1] *Zahranicni Obchod*, quoted by *Czechoslovak Economic Bulletin*, no. 29 (1946), p. 4.
[2] ibid. nos. 27, 28 (1946), p. 3, p. 3.

1945, was based not merely on a quota exchange for goods, but opened the door for deals directly agreed upon between industrial and trade organizations of both countries.

In the light of subsequent events in Czechoslovakia, it is of interest to recall in some detail the attitude of the pre-February Government towards trading with the USSR.

People in the Western countries, said Dr Ripka, often fail to understand why we are so interested that the USSR should purchase from us the largest possible quantity of our heavy industrial products. The answer is simply that our best possibilities for the sale of these goods appear to be in the USSR and in Central Europe, and not in the Western markets, owing to the high industrial capacities of those countries. The Soviet Union will be able to take many of our products whose selling price is mostly payment for man-hours of work that has gone into their fabrication, and whose export is thus peculiarly advantageous for us. We are already exporting to Russia the work of our own hands in the form of orders to our factories for goods made from raw materials delivered for that purpose, and for which payment for the goods delivered is also commonly made in raw materials.

Dr Ripka at the same time rejected any suggestions that his country's foreign trade was in any way under the control of Soviet factors. 'It would,' he said, 'on the contrary, be all to the good if the independence of our foreign trade was everywhere respected as it is in Moscow.'[1]

The Czechoslovak Government was, moreover, willing to adapt the country's industry to the needs of the USSR, confident of the economic advantages to be derived from such co-operation. 'The Soviet system of successive five-year plans will guarantee us,' declared Dr Ripka, 'provided we are prepared to co-operate suitably within the scheme of Russia's general requirements, long-term orders which we greatly need for the planning of our production, and which will guarantee continuity of employment. This will also guarantee regular sales for us, since the Soviet market is not affected by the competitive variations of the world market. Later we shall be able to deliver consumer goods, for which the demand in Russia is constantly increasing and will not be satisfied for a long period.' Belief in the relative safety of trade with the East and fear of a possible world crisis was also expressed: 'We must remember that it is not impossible that there may be a world crisis in foreign trade

[1] *Czechoslovak Economic Bulletin*, nos. 28, 29 (1946) pp. 3, 4.

which will be heavily to our loss simply because our foreign trade is directed so very largely towards the Western countries. It would be a short-sighted policy if we did not seek now to ensure ourselves against the worst of the consequences of the expected crisis by expanding our commercial relations with the USSR, and with the countries of Central and South Eastern Europe'.[1]

For the moment, however, unsatisfactory transport facilities constituted a serious hindrance to the smooth development of Czechoslovak-Soviet trade; therefore, the broad outlines of a solution to the transport problem were also discussed in Moscow during the negotiations for the commercial treaty. An agreement was finally concluded in December 1946.[2] Direct railway communication between the USSR and Czechoslovakia was envisaged crossing the Carpathians by the Jablonica Pass, and running via Čop and Mukačevo. Later the construction of a new junction system at Cerna in Roumania was reported,[3] linking the Czechoslovak railway system to that of the USSR. During the negotiations the Soviet authorities also agreed to return to the ČSR all the Danube vessels formerly the property of the Czechoslovak Danube Navigation Company, which had hitherto been used by the Soviet military authorities. Finally, the Soviet occupation authorities in Germany had put through certain administrative measures to shorten the routing of goods from Hamburg via the Elbe through German territory.[4]

Under the 1946 trade agreement various Czechoslovak trade delegations successively visited the USSR and concluded contracts with Soviet industrial organizations. It seems that at one time Czechoslovak industrialists expressed their dissatisfaction with the low-grade quality of Soviet ores. It was probably in connexion with such complaints that an agreement was negotiated for the delivery of 1,000,000 tons of ore from the USSR with an iron content of 58 per cent, at prices corresponding to those of the world market. The ore was to be delivered c.i.f., at the reloading station on the frontier of the USSR and to be paid for under the normal clearing system. Further, trans-

---

[1] Session of the Trade and Craft Committee of the Constitutional National Assembly. Reported in *Czechoslovak Economic Bulletin*, no. 57 (1946) p. 4.
[2] *The Times* (13 December 1946).
[3] *Daily Worker* (2 December 1947).
[4] *Czechoslovak Economic Bulletin*, no. 29 (1946) pp. 3, 4.

port possibilities via the Black Sea and the Danube were to be considered.[1]

The working of the trade agreements in general cannot always have been very smooth. A statement by Dr Ripka to the Trade and Craft Committee of the Constitutional National Assembly on 16 October 1946 points to the difficulties and the methods of overcoming them:

As regards commerce with the USSR, we are coming steadily to a better and more convenient working out of the various individual quotas. The planning system in use in both countries assists this end. At first goods had been exchanged more or less at random, since we had to rely chiefly upon estimates rather than concrete plans worked out in advance. Transport and transfer difficulties had, of course, caused considerable delays, so that today certain consignments were being delivered which had been agreed upon before the conclusion of the Czechoslovak-Soviet convention of 12 April 1946. It had also been necessary to clear up and overcome certain difficulties which had arisen mostly in connexion with advance consignments in connexion with which agreement on prices had been postponed; this applies to both sides.

Of the large number of consignments of Soviet goods imported in return for a simple promise to pay, Dr Ripka mentioned in particular, corn, honey, tea, oil-cakes, cotton, wool, flax, the first allocation of iron ore (250,000 tons, delivered from the ruined and half-flooded mines of Krivoi Rog), manganese and chrome ore, pyrites, and a number of other important raw materials. For most of these consignments the prices for both sides were agreed upon separately and sometimes many months after delivery. Czechoslovakia had, he continued, imported goods capable of short-term delivery, but was herself delivering chiefly machinery and other products requiring a considerable period for manufacture. Thus, for example, Soviet orders with long-term periods of delivery amounted to about a milliard Kčs, of which one-fifth had already been punctually delivered within the assigned period, while the remaining four-fifths remained on order for delivery at a later agreed date. Unbalanced debts arising from the larger Soviet consignments could thus soon be smoothed out. Czechoslovakia's indebtedness to the USSR would also be reduced by the payment of pre-war Czechoslovak claims, which the Soviet Government were gradually freeing in accordance with the convention of 12 April

[1] ibid. no. 65 (1947) p. 4.

24

1946. His summing-up was that 'experience up to the present, though relatively short, justifies the expectation that Czechoslovak-Soviet economic relations will develop more promisingly and more widely . . .'[1]

THE JULY 1947 AGREEMENT

In July 1947 another Czechoslovakian Government delegation went to Moscow to discuss relations between the two countries, with particular reference to economic questions. It was agreed to broaden economic relations 'in order to guarantee an uninterrupted and lasting exchange of goods between the two States in the interests of fulfilling the economic plans of both and of ensuring full employment'.[2] Both Governments agreed to conclude a treaty for mutual delivery of goods for a period of five years, the annual quotes to be settled in due course.

Great importance was attached by both countries to this agreement, the negotiations of which more or less coincided with the opening of the Marshall Conference in Paris (9–12 July 1947). The agreement was obviously meant to compensate Czechoslovakia for her withdrawal from the Marshall Plan.

A Soviet commentator, B. Leontiev, gave the following appraisal of the agreement: 'Having been made possible, thanks to the advantages of planned economy, this agreement will in turn assist the successful fulfilment of the five-year economic plan of the USSR and the corresponding plans of the Czechoslovak Republic.'[3] The interdependence of the two economies is here clearly indicated.

Evžen Loebl, Department Head in the Foreign Trade Ministry, stressing the advantages of the new agreement in an interview with *Rude Pravo* of 17 July[4] pointed out at the same time that it was in no way detrimental to trade with Western countries, and that, on the contrary, Czechoslovakia hoped to play her part in the reconstruction of Europe.

In September 1947 a Czechoslovak economic delegation of about 200 experts consisting of representatives of all industrial ministries and the National Bank, headed by Mr Loebl, went to Moscow to discuss details of the new commercial agreement

[1] ibid. no. 54 (1946) pp. A, B.
[2] ibid. no. 90 (1947) p. 3.
[3] 'Mezhdunarodnoe Obozrenie', *Pravda* (16 July 1947)
[4] Quoted by *Czechoslovak News Letter* (25 July 1947).

which, it was expected, would direct a considerable part of Czechoslovakia's exports to the USSR for the next five years. The delegation was to work out quotas for 1948, approximate quotas for the following four years, and to negotiate the assessment of prices. It was later to be succeeded by delegations from individual branches of industry, to work out details for delivery contracts on the broad outlines agreed upon by the Government delegation.[1]

After four months of negotiations and drafting of details, a Trade and Navigation Agreement was finally signed on 11 December 1947[2] for an unlimited period of time, implementing the 1943 Treaty of Alliance and replacing the Trade and Navigation Treaty of March 1935. Simultaneously an important commercial agreement was concluded for a period of five years. The mutual exchange of goods during this period was envisaged at some 50 milliard Kčs ($100 million) with an average annual turnover of approximately 5 milliard Kčs each way. (Subsequently, the volume of trade was increased).

The commercial agreement included a short-term Soviet loan of 1,150 million Kčs, to be paid off by Czechoslovakia in goods during the years 1949 and 1950, since in 1948 it would not be possible for Czechoslovakia to pay for Russian deliveries, including 600,000 tons of grain, by exports to the USSR. Czechoslovak exports to the USSR were to consist of products both of heavy and of light industry. The list of goods to be delivered by Czechoslovakia (one of the appendixes of the agreement) names over 200 commodities.

Definite quotas were to be agreed upon each year, on the basis of which binding contracts would be arranged between Soviet economic organizations and Czechoslovak concerns. Quotas for the smelting and machine industry were made out for the full period of five years, thus enabling the Czechoslovak industry more definitely and accurately to estimate its production plan.

'The prices', Dr Ripka explained, 'have been negotiated on the basis of world market prices, to which has been added 50 per cent of the transport costs from the world market under consideration'. This he considered in the majority of cases very

---

[1] *Neue Züricher Zeitung* (9 September 1947); *Czechoslovak Economic Bulletin*, no. 100 (1947) p. 10; no. 97 (1947) p. 8.
[2] *Vneshnaya Torgovlya*, no. 6 (1948) p. 26, and *Czechoslovak Economic Bulletin*, r.o. 111 (1947) pp. 6–9.

advantageous for Czechoslovakia. Payments would be carried out on a clearing system, under which the various export and import contracts were to be so arranged as to lead to the payments on either side being covered by mutual deliveries of goods.[1]

Both the contracting parties bind themselves, in their mutual economic relations, to give the other party the benefit of most-favoured-nation procedure, this to apply to customs, taxation, and transport facilities. The setting-up of a special trade representatives' department at the Soviet Embassy was provided for, to assist, supervise, and carry out the Czechoslovak-Soviet Trade Treaty.

Finally, an agreement on scientific and technical co-operation was concluded for the exchange of scientific and technical information and experience in the field of industrial production. To this end, a special Czechoslovak-Soviet committee was to be set up, to which each Government would nominate five members, and which would sit twice a year, alternately in Moscow and in Prague.

Orders and Deliveries for 1948

The 1948 agreement envisaged exports to the USSR to the value of 5 milliard Kčs and imports from there to the value of over 6 milliard Kčs.[2] Czechoslovakia was to supply rails, locomotives, and other railway equipment, machinery for the crude-oil industry, equipment for the sugar-making and shoe-making industries, machine tools, electro-motors, excavators, small electric power-plants, motor cars, breeding-cattle, sugar, footwear, and textile goods. Soviet deliveries to Czechoslovakia were to include 60,000 tons of potassium fertilizers, 5,000 tons of nitrogenous fertilizers, 20,000 tons of cotton, 30 tons of sunflower seed, 2,470 tons of flax seed, 2,500 tons of vetch seed, unspecified quantities of peas, lentils, wool, iron ore, manganese and chromium ores, ferro-alloys, phosphates, and—most

[1] In his book *Le Coup de Prague* (Librairie Plon, Paris, 1949) p. 132, Dr Ripka says about this trade agreement: 'On the whole, the treaty which I had just signed was advantageous for us because I was able to get certain important concessions: our exports of consumer goods were considerably increased; deliveries of special equipment for the oil fields, which the Russians had tried to force us to make in a very crude way because these articles were of strategic interest to them, were substantially reduced; prices and conditions of payment were on the whole not unfavourable and finally, I had obtained a credit of one milliard crowns, which would facilitate the settlement for imports from Russia'.

[2] *Czechoslovak Economic Bulletin*, no. 111 (1947) p. 4.

important of all—200,000 tons of wheat and 200,000 tons of fodder (grain and maize),[1] to be delivered before the end of April 1948.

The original grain deal negotiated under the July 1947 agreement, after Czechoslovakia's withdrawal from the Marshall Plan, was for 200,000 tons of bread grains, plus 200,000 tons of fodder. It soon became apparent, however, that owing to a disastrous harvest, Czechoslovakia had to reckon with a deficit of at least 300,000 tons of grain. In October 1947 the late Jan Masaryk went to the United States to obtain deliveries of grain, but was unsuccessful in his mission. The Czechoslovak Government therefore decided to approach the USSR for additional deliveries. This was finally done in a somewhat dramatic form, fully exploited by the Czech Communist press, the Premier Klement Gottwald making a personal appeal to Marshal Stalin for another 150,000 tons.[2] A cabled personal reply from Stalin on 29 November promised to double Soviet deliveries, thus bringing the total to 400,000 tons of bread grains. In his telegram Stalin was reported[3] to have stated also that the USSR was prepared to improve the terms of the Czechoslovak-Soviet Trade Agreement about to be concluded in Moscow, especially in regard to Czechoslovakia's payments for goods.

As to prices for the Soviet grain and fodder, Dr Ripka considered them extremely advantageous, and since there were no objections from the Soviet side to their publication, he gave them as follows:

Wheat (per ton)	6,100	Kčs =	$122
Rye	,,	6,279	,,	$125
Maize	,,	5,668·50	,,	$113
Barley	,,	5,107·50	,,	$102
Oats	,,	5,150·50	,,	$103

plus half the transport costs.

According to Dr Ripka the difference in price from that current in North America was 931·3 milliard Kčs for the total quantity. In the event of any purchases from Canada, the Argentine, etc., the price difference he said, might well have been as much as 1,300 to 1,700 milliard Kčs.[4]

[1] ibid. no. 90 (1947) p. 3; no. 113 (1948) p. 4.
[2] Ripka, op. cit. p. 129.   [3] *New York Times* (2 December 1947).
[4] *Czechoslovak Economic Bulletin*, no. 116 (1948) p. 11.

The deliveries from the USSR started at the beginning of December 1947 with five trainloads daily which had to be reloaded at Cerna owing to the different railway gauge.[1] It appears that the considerable transport difficulties were overcome more or less successfully, the reloading having been carried out in three shifts. By 30 April 1948 not more than 738 truckloads of wheat and 2,027 truckloads of maize remained to be delivered;[2] and in May the total quantity agreed upon was exceeded by a few trainloads. The USSR had by that time sent[3]:

Milling wheat	22,859	truckloads
Rye	15,146	,,
Barley	2,942	,,
Oats	2,000	,,
Maize	14,914	,,
Seed wheat	1,987	,,
Flax seed	202	,,
Vetch	260	,,
Sunflower seed	3	,,

The protocol for the exchange of goods for 1949 was signed in Moscow in October 1948, and provided for a very considerable increase in the trade between the two countries, raising the turnover from the originally planned 10 milliard Kčs to 18 milliard Kčs. Exports to the USSR were envisaged to the value of more than 9 milliard Kčs, imports to the value of 8·7 milliard Kčs, thus enabling the Czechoslovak Government to pay off part of the Soviet credit of 1·15 milliard Kčs granted in 1947. Prices were said to be based on 'the principle of price stability, i.e. on the preceding year's prices or on world market prices for commodities which were not previously included, as well as for Soviet grain and seed, and Czechoslovak hops and sugar.'[4] The goods to be exchanged in 1949 included in particular the following:

EXPORTS TO THE U.S.S.R.

Leather boots and light footwear	Kčs	1,300	million
Rubber footwear	,,	690	,,
Cotton fabrics	,,	750	,,
Other fabrics, as well as ready-made clothing	,,	210	,,
Knitted wear and hosiery	,,	150	,,
Zip fasteners	,,	45	,,
Textile machinery	,,	66	,,
Artificial leather	,,	70	,,

[1] *Volksstimme* (12 December 1947).
[2] *Czechoslovak Economic Bulletin*, no. 131 (1948) p. 5.
[3] ibid. no. 132 (1948) p. 7.   [4] ibid. no. 152 (1948) pp. 3, 5.

EXPORTS TO THE U.S.S.R.—continued

Heavy engineering products (locomotives, motor cars, electric installations, dredgers, motors, etc.)	Kčs	1 milliard
Foundry output: (tubes, rails, wheels, tin-plate, etc.)	,,	1·2 ,,
Window glass	6,000,000 metres	
Cigarette paper	1,500 tons	
Parchment paper	800 ,,	
Porcelain ware	500–700 ,,	
Lorries	200	
Passenger cars	50	
Pencils	100,000 gross	
Hops	500 tons	
Sugar	60,000 ,,	

IMPORTS FROM THE U.S.S.R.

Wheat	300,000 tons
Fats	25,000 ,,
Meat	25,000 ,,
Barley	20,000 ,,
Sunflower seeds, lentils, peas, and seed for flax and hemp	15,000 ,,
Iron ore	800,000 ,,
Iron scrap	100,000 ,,
Raw cotton	45,000 ,,

Manganese and chrome ores, manganite, asbestos, phosphates, petroleum distillates, flax-tow, ball-bearings, lead, electrolytic copper, nickel, salt, sulphur, nitrate fertilizers, ash logs, oak staves, etc. were also imported

The USSR also undertook to supply 1,500 tons of wool, 300 tons of camel-hair, 500 tons of flax-tow, 150 tons of jute, 60 tons of animal hair, and rabbit skins, to the value of 50 milliard Kčs for the hat-making industry.[1]

The total value of raw materials to be imported from the USSR in 1949 was estimated at some 5 milliard Kčs. Raw cotton will account for 4·5 milliard Kčs, 'the largest sum ever spent under a single trade agreement in the history of Czechoslovakia's foreign trade'. (A contract for 35,000 tons was concluded in December 1948, and another 10,000 tons were negotiated by Premier Klement Gottwald during his visit to the Crimea in September 1948. Of the spun cotton only about 9 per cent will now have to be re-exported to the USSR.)

A noteworthy feature was the change in the range of goods. The emphasis for 1949 is on the import from Russia of more raw materials, chiefly at the expense of foodstuffs, and on increased exports to the USSR of light industry goods, instead of capital goods. It was perhaps for the purpose of stimulating

[1] *Czechoslovak Economic Bulletin*, no. 161 (1948) pp. 12, 13.

Soviet interest that an exhibition of Czechoslovak light industry goods was held in Moscow in July-August 1948.

The import of foodstuffs from the USSR was to fall from 62 per cent in 1948 to 40 per cent in 1949; that of finished goods (equipment for mines, power stations, film studios, etc.) from 6 to 3 per cent. The import of raw materials, on the other hand, was to increase from 32 to 57 per cent. Czechoslovakia's exports to the Soviet Union were to show the following changes: the share of light industry goods to rise from 49 per cent in 1948 to 70 in 1949; the products of the foundry and engineering trade to fall from 41 to 25 per cent and that of agricultural produce from 10 to 5 per cent.[1]

This trend (extended imports of raw materials from the USSR and increased exports of consumer goods to Russia) has been further developed by an agreement signed in February 1949[2] extending the original total trade turnover (of approximately $354 million) by another 2 milliard Kčs ($40 million). The total Czechoslovak trade turnover with the USSR in 1949 was to be about 45 per cent higher than in 1948. The goods additionally to be delivered by Russia were to comprise non-ferrous metals, iron ore, ball bearings, buna rubber. It is probable that, owing to the blockade of Yugoslavia, which was an important source, particularly of such raw materials as copper and lead, Czechoslovak industry is experiencing difficulties (though trade relations with Yugoslavia were not actually broken off by the Czech Government until June 1949). It is also possible that some of them are caused by the ban imposed by the United States on the export of war potential goods. Whether the USSR will be in a position to satisfy the needs of the Czechoslovak industry is an open question. While during the years immediately following the end of the war Soviet deliveries of raw materials seem to have been prompt and satisfactory,[3] probably chiefly for political reasons, growing difficulties and delays were noticeable in the later years.[4] The exclusion of Yugoslavia from commercial relations with the Cominform countries can only add to their economic and trade difficulties.

In July 1949, on the occasion of the second Czechoslovak industrial exhibition in Moscow (this time of both light and

---

[1] ibid. no. 155 (1948) pp. 4, 5.
[2] *New York Herald Tribune* (12 February 1949).
[3] *Czechoslovak Economic Bulletin*, no. 60 (1946) pp. 7-8.
[4] Ripka, op. cit. p. 132, and *The Times* (29 July 1949).

heavy industry goods, which was given considerable prominence in the Soviet press), an agreement was concluded for the delivery before the end of 1949 of Soviet capital goods to the value of 250 million Kčs, and further deliveries in 1950.[1] A further 'expansion of the mutual exchange of goods and economic co-operation' was also discussed by the Czech delegation and the Soviet Government. Whether this general statement of policy will become a reality will depend on economic factors within the two countries as well as on their relations with the West. The questions at issue are: Will the USSR be able to satisfy the growing needs of Czechoslovakian industry for raw materials? Will Czechoslovakia succeed in strengthening her commercial ties with the Western countries, and will she have sufficient and interesting enough export surpluses to pay for her imports? Will the increased exports to Russia of consumer goods become a permanent feature of Czechoslovakian foreign trade, thus freeing heavy industry goods for delivery to the other Eastern European countries, and partly to the Western world? These questions cannot as yet be answered definitely. Since the 1947 agreement, trade with the USSR has tended to increase, with emphasis on growing imports of raw materials and rising exports of light industry goods. This, however, has not, so far, impaired trade either with the other Eastern European countries or with the rest of the world, since Czechoslovak foreign trade is, on the whole, still expanding. The five-year plan provides for a further increase in the volume of trade by 40 per cent as against 1948 and no intention has so far been noticeable to reduce trade with the Western world.

[1] *New York Times* (12 July 1949). Note: As will be seen later, the USSR has also undertaken to deliver capital goods to Poland and Hungary. It seems most unlikely that she can do this from her own production. She is, in all probability, re-exporting equipment and machinery bought or received from other countries, chiefly Germany.

Chapter Three

POLAND

NEXT to the USSR, Poland probably suffered the greatest destruction by war, having twice been made a battlefield. The military operations during winter and spring 1944–5 in particular must have considerably damaged her industry and agriculture. But the occupation of the country in 1939–40 by Germany and the USSR, and from 1941 onwards by Germany alone, equally had an effect on her economy, and we see indeed that the industry of the *General Gouvernement*, like that of other Eastern European countries, was disrupted and adapted to the needs of Germany's war economy, regardless of its pre-war structure. Part of Polish industrial equipment was, moreover, removed to Germany; many industrial enterprises were closed down while others were allowed to deteriorate beyond repair. When the war ended, Poland's economy was in a state of complete anarchy.

EFFECT OF TERRITORIAL CHANGES ON FOREIGN TRADE

Immediately after the war the situation was further aggravated by big territorial changes and a large-scale transfer of population, both of which meant radical changes in the country's economy and consequently its foreign trade. The total area of Poland was reduced by 20 per cent and its total population—as a result of war losses and transfer—by over 30 per cent. In the east Poland has, through cession to the USSR, lost about 17 per cent of her forest area. This will greatly reduce Poland's timber exports, which, before the war, constituted 25 per cent of her total exports. The loss of large stretches of agricultural land is, on the other hand, not expected to reduce the country's agricultural production since the newly acquired territories in the west are more productive than those transferred to the USSR, and the new Poland should, after rehabilitation, produce as much as pre-war Poland.

With the acquisition of her new territories in the west, Poland has gained: first, about 312 miles of coastline with the

33

important port of Szczecin (Stettin), the river Oder, and the canal and rail network of the area; second, the Silesian coal-fields, the largest known coal resources in Europe (said to be even larger than those of the Ruhr or the Don); and third, the entire industrial area of Upper and Lower Silesia with their great resources of power, minerals, and various industries such as ceramic, cement, glass, cotton, flax, electro-technical and chemical works, photographic, optical, medical equipment works, paper-mills, food processing plants, and saw-mills. These gains will more than double her industrial potential since, although she has lost 71 per cent of her crude oil and all potassium salts, gains of other raw materials are considerable, namely, zinc and lead 146·8 per cent (of her 1937 production), coke 152, coal 78·6, and steel 48·6 per cent; lignite increased 421 times, compared with 1937.[1]

It is obvious that, as a consequence of these changes, Poland's foreign trade will in future be very different from that of pre-war years. In fact it has changed already. When analysing her post-war foreign trade it is necessary, however, to distinguish between changes of a temporary nature caused by the necessity of immediate rehabilitation and reconstruction, and funda-mental and permanent changes caused by the large-scale trans-fer of territory and population. The first feature was common to all war-devastated or war-affected countries and was reflected to a greater or smaller degree in their foreign trade during 1945–6. The second feature is—in Eastern Europe—peculiar to Poland, and the effect on her foreign trade only began to emerge towards the end of 1947. Its full effect will probably not be realized until the new territories have been completely absorbed.

A statistical comparison of Poland's present-day foreign trade with that of the pre-war years is difficult for two reasons: first, no analysis would be accurate that did not take into account the territorial changes; second, such Polish statistical data as are available use different nomenclature at different times.[2] In both instances rather complicated adjustments would be required to get a clear picture, which would be outside the scope of this study. All that can be indicated here is the trend

---

[1] Unrra, OAP, no. 35 (1947) *Industrial Rehabilitation in Poland* (revised) p. 6, and no. 40 *Foreign Trade of Poland* (revised) p. 6.

[2] Compare Polish exports and imports in *Wiadomości Statystyczne*, no. 5 (1947) pp. 63–64, and no. 11 (1948) pp. 154–6.

of Polish foreign trade in general as outlined for example in an article in *Vneshnaya Torgovlya*.[1] It was stated that in view of the great changes in Poland's economy, timber and agricultural products could not be exported at all, except for so-called luxury agricultural products such as eggs and bacon. Poland's most important export commodities had become coal and coke,[2] cement and zinc, while the export of textiles and other manufactured goods is developing. In 1947 fats and other foodstuffs still had to be imported, but the import of grain was to cease by the end of that year, and the import of all foodstuffs in the course of 1948 and 1949. (In 1948 the export of bacon, game, etc., had already risen to 15 per cent of the total.) Instead, a considerable increase in the imports of raw materials, auxiliary materials, and equipment was envisaged. This presupposes increased trade with both the USSR and the West.[3] A substantial part of raw materials (cotton, flax, ores, and oil products) is obtained from the USSR, but for plant and equipment Poland has to look chiefly to the West. Consequently, one argues, the less raw materials have to be imported from the West, the more foreign currency will be available for the purchase of machinery. Increased imports of raw materials from the USSR, on the other hand, will help to increase output, the standard of living, and foreign trade in general.

REORGANIZATION OF NATIONAL ECONOMY

Poland's post-war economy is a combination of State and privately owned enterprises. An Act passed in January 1946 provided the legal basis for the nationalization of key industries and all factories in other industries employing over fifty people on one shift. Small-scale works, enterprises owned by municipalities, co-operatives, and a few others were exempt from nationalization. On the basis of this Act the nationalized sector of industry was to employ about 10 per cent of all occupations, (or 25 per cent of all occupations excluding agriculture, or about

---

[1] no. 1 (1947) p. 27.

[2] *Soviet Monitor* (22 June 1948) stated that with an export of 5,779,000 tons of coal in the first quarter of 1948 Poland has become the biggest exporter in Europe, and second on the world market only to the U.S.A. According to *Vneshnaya Torgovlya*, no. 3 (1949) p. 30, the export of coal in 1946 and 1947 constituted 64 to 67 per cent of the total; in 1948 the volume had further increased but the share of coal exports diminished to 50 per cent of the total.

[3] Andrzej Kaduszkiewicz, 'The Tendencies of Poland's Postwar Trade Agreements', *Yearbook of the Foreign Trade of Poland 1948* (Warsaw) p. xxxv.

40 per cent of the entire manufacturing industry). Simultaneously with the nationalization Act a Bill decreeing the setting up of new enterprises and the encouragement of private initiative in industry and commerce was passed. It was consequently anticipated that even by the end of the four-year plan, in 1949, the number of workers in the nationalized industry would not rise above 25 per cent of all occupations, while the share of agricultural workers would have fallen to 50 per cent, leaving about 25 per cent of workers in private enterprises.[1] Agriculture is, up to the present, still run largely on the basis of private ownership following a land reform decreed on 6 September 1944, although an intensive collectivization drive was launched in the summer of 1949.

The four-year economic plan for 1946 to 1949[2] was adopted by the Polish Government for the purpose of rehabilitation and development of the country's economy. The emphasis was on rehabilitation; by the end of 1949 agricultural production (with stress on farm produce) was not expected to be more than 80 per cent and industrial production not more than 70 per cent of the pre-war level within the present boundaries of Poland. That meant an industrial output 52 per cent higher than that of pre-war Poland and 228 per cent of the output within the present boundaries in 1946. The total investment for the years 1947–9 was envisaged at $3,150 million, of which 24 per cent was to be financed by imports not paid for by Poland's exports, chiefly of capital equipment, on credit. The total required imports for 1947–9 were estimated at $1,950 million, of which only $169 million were to represent imports for direct consumption; exports for the same period were planned at only $1,183 million (of which $830 million were to represent coal exports), leaving a balance of $767 million.[3]

A new six-year plan which Polish officials are planning on the assumption of increased trade with the West to be accompanied by short and medium term credits[4] is due to start in 1950.

---

[1] 'The Nationalization of Industry in Poland', speech by the Minister of Industry, Hilary Minc, at the Ninth Session of the National Council of the Homeland. (Warsaw, The State Publishing Institute, 1946); Unrra, OAP, no. 35, op. cit. p. 35.

[2] Sometimes called three-year plan since it was not finally adopted until the beginning of 1947.

[3] Unrra, OAP, no. 35, op. cit. p. 15.

[4] 'Polish Trade and the West', *The Economist* (5 June 1948) p. 932.

ORGANIZATION AND DIRECTION OF FOREIGN TRADE

The entire foreign trade organization is in the hands of the Ministry of Industry and Commerce, which negotiates commercial agreements with other countries and issues import and export licences to Polish enterprises. In accordance with the mixed economy of the country foreign trade is conducted by State, co-operative, and private enterprises, as well as by those with mixed capital. All these operate by virtue of foreign trade concessions granted by the Ministry of Industry and Commerce. The State enterprises engaged in foreign trade (at the beginning of 1949 numbering thirty-five) are the central supplies and sales offices of the Central Boards of the individual industries, sometimes assisted by the few existing limited liability companies and one stock company. Certain co-operatives are licensed to export and import goods and these act through the Department for Foreign Trade of Spolem (co-operatives). Finally, a number of private firms are allowed to conduct foreign trade either through the State enterprises or direct with firms abroad, and their transactions are controlled by the Ministry by means of export and import licences.[1]

'One of the most important features in Poland's foreign trade', to quote an Unrra report, 'is the emergence of the USSR as one of Poland's leading trade partners'.[2] The report warns, however, that this importance should not be over-estimated.

It should be remembered that trade with the USSR began before the end of hostilities when the Polish Government was still cut off from contacts with the West and at a time when conditions in the country were still chaotic. At the time, the problem facing the Polish Government was not so much the difficulty of obtaining supplies on favourable terms, as the getting of any supplies at all. Apart from the USSR there were no alternative sources for such essential commodities as iron ore, wool, cotton, and petrol. Equally, no country but the USSR was in a position to take delivery of coal from Polish pitheads (practically the only export which Poland had to offer in exchange) in its own transport at a time when Polish railway transport was practically non-existent. . . As other means of financing Poland's rehabilitation are found the share of trade with the USSR will diminish even further. Nevertheless it will remain an important factor. The Soviet Union is the nearest source of textile raw ma-

[1] Based on 'The Co-operatives and Foreign Trade', by Dr Jan Zieleniewski, p. xlii, and 'The Foreign Trade Organization of Poland', p. 1, in *Yearbook of the Foreign Trade of Poland 1948* (Warsaw).
[2] Unrra, OAP, no. 40, op. cit. pp. 30-1.

terials, hides, furs, fertilizers, petrol, manganese, ores, and timber, all of which Poland needs urgently. If the cost of overland transport can be kept at a reasonable level, the USSR may also prove the cheapest source of supply.[1] On the other hand, the USSR too will be hard pressed by the enormous task of reconstruction, repair, and further industrialization which confronts her, and Poland cannot look to the USSR for much of the capital equipment required for her reconstruction of industry. The foundations at least for mutually satisfactory trade in good volume are clearly present, though Poland's great needs for industrial and transport equipment mean that, in the next few years, the proportion of her imports received from the USSR will rapidly diminish.

This seems to be a correct summing up of the situation, which is borne out by the following table[2]:

	1936–8 (yearly average)	1945	1946	1947	1948
			(excluding Unrra deliveries,)		
EXPORTS					
in million $	215	37	133	251	513
			PERCENTAGE OF TOTAL		
U.S.S.R.	0·4	93·4	49·6	27·9	18·9
Eastern Europe	6·0	0·7	6·1	11·1	15·4 (including Yugoslavia 4·3)
U.K.	19·3	–	1·8	2·4	6·8
U.S.A.	6·8	–	0·3	0·4	0·4
Germany (including Austria for 1938)	19·5	–	5·8	11·1	11·1
IMPORTS					
in million $	224	34	138	393	498
			PERCENTAGE OF TOTAL		
U.S.S.R.	1·1	90·7	70·3	20·1	22·8
Eastern Europe	5·4	0·0	4·0	6·6	19·4 (including Yugoslavia 5·4)
U.K.	12·3	–	0·6	7·8	5·4
U.S.A.	12·0	–	1·1	26·9	10·2
Germany (including Austria for 1938)	19·2	–	5·2	2·3	6·6

The table shows that before the war Poland's predominant trade partner was Germany, the United Kingdom and the

[1] It may be noted here that Polish exports to the USSR invariably go by rail, whereas imports from distant parts of the Soviet Union to Poland are mainly carried by sea (which often results in long delivery times, since the harbours are ice-bound part of the year). Kaduszkiewicz, op. cit. p. xxix.

[2] Sources: *Wiadomości Statystyczne*, no. 5 (1947) pp. 62, 3 (for 1936–46); *Economic Survey of Europe in 1948*, Economic Commission for Europe, Geneva 1949. Table XVI for 1947 and 1948. (This Survey will henceforth be referred to as the ECE Report). Soviet sources give total exports for 1948 at 528·6 and total imports at 515·0 million dollars and the share of the USSR at 21·9 and 24 per cent respectively (*Vneshnaya Torgovlya*, no 9 (1949) pp. 3, 4). The article in question states at the same time that Soviet trade turnover with Poland has in 1948 increased by 47 per cent compared with 1947.

United States occupying second and third places. Trade with the USSR in 1936–8 was negligible (0·4 per cent of Poland's exports and 1·1 of her imports), as was that of the other Eastern European countries except Czechoslovakia, which took 4·2 of Poland's exports and supplied 3·4 per cent of her imports.

In 1945 the position had changed very much. The Soviet Union supplied 90·7 per cent of Poland's imports and purchased 93·4 per cent of her exports, but Poland's total trade turnover for that year amounted to a mere 16·6 per cent of the 1936–8 average. In 1946 it had risen to 61·8 per cent. Soviet imports from Poland had, in money value, nearly doubled and her exports to Poland more than trebled, but her share in Poland's total exports and imports had fallen to 49·6 and 70·3 per cent respectively.

While in 1947 the USSR was still Poland's most important trade partner, long-term agreements were concluded with Yugoslavia and Czechoslovakia; the latter country in 1948 occupied second place in the foreign trade of Poland. Trade with the West in 1948[1] was also on the increase (particularly with Sweden, Finland, and Great Britain).

An analysis of Polish foreign trade after 1947 on the basis of Polish sources proved impossible, since *Wiadomości Statystyczne* has discontinued the publication of trade statistics by countries and by value, now showing foreign trade only by volume of commodities. According to the ECE Report for 1948 (Table XVI) only 34·2 per cent of Poland's total exports and 42·2 per cent of her imports were with the Eastern area. In 1949 trade with the USSR was expected to rise by 35 per cent.

TRADE WITH THE USSR

Economic relations with the USSR developed in detail on the following lines: in January 1945 the Lublin Committee, formed in opposition to the Polish Government-in-exile in London, was recognized by the Soviet Union as the Provisional Government of Poland. On 21 April 1945 a treaty of friendship, mutual assistance and post-war collaboration was signed in Moscow.[2] A frontier and reparations agreement followed on 16 August 1945. According to this Poland was to receive 15 per cent of all reparations obtained by the USSR from her zone

[1] *Vneshnaya Torgovlya*, no. 11 (1948) pp. 9–10.
[2] ibid. nos. 4–5 (1945) p. 10.

of occupation, and 15 per cent of the reparations due to the USSR from the Western zone. In return for this industrial equipment the USSR demanded delivery, at a special price, of certain quantities of coal, namely, 8 million tons in 1946, 13 million tons in each of the years 1947–50, and 12 million tons per annum thereafter throughout the occupation of Germany.[1] (In March 1947 these quantities were reduced by 50 per cent.)

The first two trade agreements between the USSR and Poland were concluded in July 1945. At least one of them contained a most-favoured-nation clause. One of the agreements was concluded to the total value of 595 million gold zloty ($186 million). Poland's chief export items to the USSR were to be 5 million metric tons of coal and coke (over and above the coal deliveries against reparation goods), iron and steel, cement, soda, etc; the USSR was to supply iron, manganese, and chrome-ores (280,750 metric tons), 40,000 tons of apatites, 25,000 tons of cotton, 17,000 tons of cellulose, 150 tractors, 1,350 automobiles, 100,000 animal hides, and other goods. Deliveries from both sides were to be made before December 1945.[2]

No details have become known about the second July agreement, except that it was concluded for an exchange of goods to the total value of 190 million gold zloty ($59 million).[4] According to foreign press reports contracts for the delivery of 2,000 Soviet locomotives and of Soviet oil to Poland were concluded in September and November 1945, possibly as supplements to the second July agreement. By mid-December Poland had also received 38,000 tons of petroleum and 9,000 tons of gasoline.[3]

A third trade treaty was signed on 12 April 1946 to remain in force until 31 March 1947, for an exchange of goods to the value of $96 million on each side. Soviet deliveries were to consist almost exclusively of grain and fodder (a total of 417,500

---

[1] *New York Herald Tribune* (17 August 1945); *The Times* (8 August 1945). Mr Mikolajczik in his book *The Pattern of Soviet Domination* (Sampson Low, 1948) p. 158, quotes a price of $1.25 a ton offered by Russia (as against $12 and $16 offered by Sweden and Denmark respectively). He does not, however, specify whether this extremely low price refers only to deliveries under the reparations agreement as indeed it seems to do. The *International Financial Statistics* (March 1949) p. 163, states that in 1946 total Polish exports included $57 million for 5·7 million tons of coal shipped to the USSR. This would amount to $10 per ton.
[2] Unrra, OAP, no. 40, op. cit. p. 63.
[4] ibid. p. 62. The total figures for the agreements, both zloty and dollars, were taken from the above quoted Unrra Report, p. 38. It is not known what rate of exchange was used, the official pre-war rate having been $1 = 5·265 gold zloty.
[3] *Neue Zürischer Zeitung* (14 September and 15 November 1945).

metric tons), and Polish exports were to include 1,300,000 tons of coal and coke, 520,000 tons of cement, 30,000 tons of iron and steel, chemicals, and other manufactures.[1]

Details of the commodities exchanged between Poland and the USSR in 1945–6 are given in *Wiadomości Statystyczne*. (Spcial Volume I, 1947, pp. 10–13.) Poland's chief exports to the USSR in 1946, in the order of money value, were: coal and coke, textiles, sugar, iron and steel products, cement. This is the last detailed statistical information available on trade with the USSR, later statistics analysing trade only by commodities.

An agreement on economic and military aid was signed in Moscow on 5 March 1947. The economic part of the agreement provided for an interest-free gold loan to Poland amounting to $28–9 million for purchases abroad (chiefly from the United States) of machinery and food. The agreement also provided for the immediate handing over by the USSR of rolling stock captured during the war, and increased Soviet supplies of modern arms and military equipment on credit. For the first time scientific and technical co-operation in the sphere of industrial production was also foreseen; Polish coal supplies under the 1945 'reparations' agreement were to be reduced in 1947 from 13 to 6·5 million tons.[2] The Soviet Union also undertook immediately to hand over to Poland her share of the German merchant fleet. Finally, the agreement dealt with problems of reparation and with the rebuilding of the wide-gauge railway line Katowice-Lwow to the Central European standard gauge.[3]

On 26 May 1947 a communiqué, issued in Warsaw after the return of a Polish Government delegation from Moscow, announced the conclusion of a comprehensive agreement covering (1) the annulment of Polish financial obligations which had arisen during the war in connexion with the arming and supplying of Polish forces by the USSR; (2) the supply of arms and munitions for the Polish army on long-term credits, pending the building up of Poland's own arms manufacturing industry: (3) credits to Poland from the USSR's gold reserves; (4) the speeding up of Soviet deliveries to Poland. Trade relations were said to have also been discussed.[4]

---

[1] Unrra, OAP, no. 40, op. cit. p. 64.　　[2] See p. 40.
[3] *The Times*; *Manchester Guardian* (7 March 1947).
[3] ibid.; ibid. (28 May 1946).

A new short-term trade agreement was concluded on 4 August 1947.[1] On this no authentic details could be obtained, but according to the daily press it seems to have provided for big cuts in deliveries of Silesian coal to the Soviet Union (deliveries were now expected to be less than 2 million tons a year), thus freeing coal for the European market. Another feature was the import of Soviet equipment for the prospecting of oil-fields and deep borings in Polish Pomerania.[2] Other goods to be exchanged were, according to the *Moscow News* (6 August 1947), non-ferrous metals, cotton fabrics, sugar, coke, window glass, etc., to be supplied by Poland in exchange for Soviet iron and manganese ore, ferro-alloys, oil products, apatites, chemicals, and other goods and, according to the *Manchester Guardian* (7 August 1947), 50,000 tons of raw cotton (70 per cent of Poland's requirements in 1946). Of the raw cotton only 17 per cent was to be reexported to the USSR as finished goods, covering 65 per cent of the cost of the raw cotton. Details as to prices, quantities, and manner of payment have apparently not been disclosed.

The conclusion of an additional agreement for 300,000 tons of grain from the Soviet Union was reported by *Volksstimme* (6 September 1947), the first delivery to be made in September 1947, the rest before the end of the year.

This pact was signed during the Marshall Plan Conference in Paris and, according to the *Soviet Monitor* (5 August 1947), it was then decided to begin negotiations in the near future for a long-term trade agreement. These negotiations were indeed opened and resulted in the signing on 26 January 1948 of a five-year agreement on mutual goods deliveries for the period 1948–52 to a total value of over $1,000 million.[3] As before, the Soviet Union intends to exchange iron, chromium and manganese ores, oil products, cotton, aluminium, asbestos, automobiles, tractors, and other goods, for Polish coal and coke, textile goods, sugar, zinc, steel goods, railway rolling stock, cement. Prices are to be fixed annually on the basis of world prices. The annual quotas of the basic goods to be exchanged are laid down by the agreement; details are to be defined three months before the beginning of each year.[4]

Simultaneously an agreement was signed for the delivery to

---

[1] *Soviet Monitor* (5 August 1948).   [2] The *Observer* (3 August 1947).
[3] *Soviet Monitor* (27 January 1948).
[4] *Vneshnaya Torgovlya*, no. 4 (1948) p. 12.

Poland during the period 1948–56 of industrial equipment (in particular for big new metallurgical plants), of equipment for power stations, for chemical plants (nitrogen-fertilizers, soda, carbide), as well as equipment for the metal-working, textile and other industries, and equipment for the restoration of towns and ports. To cover the cost of these deliveries the Soviet Union granted Poland a medium-term credit of up to $450 million. In an interview published in *Zycie Warszawy* of 10 August 1948 the head of the Treaties Department of the Ministry of Foreign Trade, Mr Rozanski, revealed that the plans for the various plants would be drawn by the USSR and that Soviet technical and economic experts would assist in the erection of the equipment. Under the same agreement, the USSR was to deliver to Poland 200,000 tons of grain, bringing the total for the agricultural year 1947–8 to 500,000 tons. The additional 200,000 tons were to be delivered within three months from the signing of the agreement.

The joint Soviet-Polish communique[1] also stated that 'during the negotiations questions relating to the implementation of the agreement of 5 March 1947 concerning technical co-operation were also examined, as well as questions relating to the deliveries of the Polish share of German reparations in 1948.'

The extent of the five-year trade agreement, which will increase the volume of trade between the two countries by 30–35 per cent, is clearly meant, as in the case of Czechoslovakia, to be a compensation for Poland's non-participation in the Marshall Plan and is intended to enable Poland to expand her industry and agriculture according to her economic plans.

Mr Minc, the Polish Minister of Industry, in a press statement (*The Times* 31 January 1948) explained that the credit of $450 million was granted for ten years in the form of capital goods and raw materials, excluding war materials; it was repayable in goods at a 3 per cent rate of interest. He also said— a statement which conflicts with the Soviet-Polish communiqué on the agreement—that the Soviet Union would henceforth not receive any coal from Poland apart from the 6·5 million tons per annum of 'reparation' coal,[2] leaving it to Poland to sell the coal to the West in order to obtain machinery which the USSR could not supply.

---

[1] *Soviet Monitor* loc. cit.   [2] See p. 41.

According to a report in *The Times* (3 February 1948), about one third of the loan is to be used for the erection of a large iron and steel plant capable of producing 1·5 million tons of iron and 1 million tons of steel per year, which would almost double Poland's steel production and greatly increase her iron output. Erection was to start early in the spring of 1949; the USSR was to supply all necessary materials and, if desired, technical assistance and supervision. *Inter alia*, the USSR was also to supply a complete motor car assembly plant in which Russian manufactured car parts could be assembled in large quantities.

Mr Minc's comment[1] on the agreement was on the familiar propaganda lines that under the Marshall Plan Poland would have received consumer goods of varying qualities and usefulness. Under the agreement with the USSR Poland would receive capital goods which should enable her to develop her industrial potential, to produce consumer goods, intensify her agriculture, and consequently, in the long run, increase her trade turnover with other countries. He added that the Soviet loan was given without any political conditions and that Poland did not have to deposit an equivalent sum in zloty as would have been the case had she accepted Marshall aid. The army newspaper *Polska Zbroina* consoled its readers with the statement that Poland was better off with the $450 million credit from the USSR than with the requested, but not granted, loan of $600 million from the International Monetary Fund, since she would now receive 'neither horsemeat conserves, nor powdered omelets, but investment goods for industrial reconstruction'.[2]

Within the framework of the five-year agreement a trade pact for 1948 was signed in May 1948 to the value of $110 million each way, exceeding the total turnover originally foreseen by $20 million. (The actual turnover figure reached is stated to be $228·7 million.) The list of goods does include coal—contrary to Mr Minc's statement—the explanation apparently being that Polish coal production was expected to exceed the 1948 target of 67·5 million tons, and that an additional 750,000 tons of mixed coal were included to balance deliveries of $21 million worth of grain received in 1946–7 and listed as a debt item for 1948. (It is also possible that Poland was unable to place her

[1] *Polish Facts and Figures* (7 February 1948).
[2] ibid. (4 June 1949).

44

coal export surpluses with Western countries.) The USSR is expected to deliver 65,000 tons of cotton and over 500,000 tons of iron ore.[1] Surveying Poland's economic and trade position, *Vneshnaya Torgovlya*[2] writes that in 1948 the USSR supplied Poland with 43 per cent of all imported iron ore, 100 per cent of manganese and chrome ore, 72 per cent of all imported cotton, 57 per cent of grain, 45 per cent of oil products, as well as with large quantities of machinery, apparatus, equipment, and instruments. Poland, on the other hand, delivered to the USSR 29 per cent of all her coal and coke exports, 15 per cent of all exported ferrous metals, 50 per cent of zinc and zinc sheets, 47 per cent of cement, 69 per cent of textile goods, 55 per cent of all exported sugar, as well as increased quantities of consumer goods, such as glass, chinaware, and others.

A further expansion of Soviet-Polish trade was envisaged by the protocol signed on 15 January 1949 which, covering the same range of goods, was to amount to about 715 million roubles each way.[3] This represents an increase of about 35 per cent over the turnover anticipated when the five-year agreement was concluded in 1947. The total for 1949 should thus amount to approximately $135 million. It is unlikely, however, that Poland's trade with all the Eastern countries will in 1949 have surpassed 50 per cent of her total trade turnover; a considerable percentage, roughly £30 million a year, will be directed to, and come from, Great Britain under a five-year trade and financial agreement concluded in 1949.

It may be recalled that the same trend, increased purchases of consumer goods on the part of the USSR, features in the current Soviet-Czechoslovak agreement. This is an interesting point, since before the war, the Soviet Union, owing to currency considerations, used to cut the import of consumer goods to the utmost. This is still true today in her trade with the West. Increased imports of consumer goods from her satellite countries show that, on the one hand, the Soviet Government feels compelled to meet to a greater extent the never yet fully satisfied needs of the Russian population, which have obviously further grown since the war; on the other hand, she can do this now far more advantageously (from a currency point of view) than hitherto, owing to her economic and political hold over the

---

[1] *Financial Times* (25 May 1948).   [2] No. 9 (1949) p. 3.
[3] *Soviet Monitor* (17 January 1949).

Eastern European countries. It is hereby not suggested that this trend is entirely disadvantageous for the countries concerned, since in the given circumstances they would hardly be able to dispose of their manufactured goods in the West.

Chapter Four

BULGARIA

BULGARIA, in regard to post-war economic relations with the USSR, occupies an intermediate position between the war-time allies, Czechoslovakia and Poland, and the conquered enemy States, Hungary and Roumania. Accordingly, Bulgaria neither enjoys the relative economic independence which the first two countries still do to a certain extent, nor has it been incorporated into and exploited by the Soviet economy to the same degree as the last two.

Although Bulgaria was under German occupation from the beginning of March 1941 and at war with the United Kingdom and the United States, she remained neutral in regard to the USSR until 5 September 1944, when the latter declared war on her. Within a few hours the Bulgarian Government asked for an armistice, and in turn declared war on Germany on 9 September 1944, the day when the Red Army entered Bulgaria. The armistice agreement with the USSR, the United States, and the United Kingdom was concluded on 28 September 1944. The Peace Treaty was signed in Paris on 2 February 1947.[1] Reparation claims were made only on behalf of Yugoslavia and Greece, initially to the value of $75 million; later this claim was reduced. The country was, however, obliged to pay the costs for the Soviet troops, whose withdrawal from Bulgaria was not completed until 14 December 1947.

CHANGES IN FOREIGN TRADE AND NATIONAL ECONOMY

Before the war Bulgaria had trade relations (including an extensive transit trade) with nearly all European, and some overseas countries. The chief place was occupied by Germany. On the eve of the war the foreign trade of Bulgaria presented the following picture.

Out of total imports in 1938 of 60 million gold dollars, 52 per cent came from Germany and Austria; 18 per cent from Eastern European countries (Czechoslovakia, Hungary, Poland,

[1] Cmd. 7022, p. 103.

Roumania, Yugoslavia, USSR), and 30 per cent from all other countries. On the export side (with a total of $68 million) the corresponding percentages were 59, 12, and 29.

Bulgaria's chief exports were foodstuffs (49·8 per cent of the total in 1938) and tobacco (42·5 per cent). The chief import items were chemicals, textiles, metals, machinery, which in 1938 together accounted for 77·9 per cent of the total.[1]

Germany's predominant position in Bulgaria's foreign trade was in 1945 taken by the USSR, though in the subsequent years the latter's share declined as will be seen from the following table featuring the changes in the direction of trade from 1945 onwards[2]:

EXPORTS

	1938	1945	1946	1947	1948 Jan.–May
			in ooo leva		
Total:	$62 million	12,397,000	14,942,000	24,532,740	12,127,909
		PERCENTAGE OF TOTAL			
Germany	56·5	0·5	0·2	0·4	3·0
U.S.S.R.	0·0	95·2	66·0	51·9	41·5
Eastern Europe	1·1	2·3	17·0	33·7	34·2
U.K.	3·2	–	0·5	0·1	0·3
U.S.A.	3·2	–	5·2	6·0	0·2

IMPORTS

	1938	1945	1946	1947	1948 Jan.–May
			in ooo leva		
Total:	$46 million	5,820,000	17,514,000	21,415,418	16,968,786
		PERCENTAGE OF TOTAL			
Germany	50·0	6·3	0·4	0·3	1·2
U.S.S.R.	0·0	79·6	81·9	60·6	58·9
Eastern Europe	1·7	6·8	8·8	26·9	26·2
U.K.	2·2	0·0	0·0	0·7	1·0
U.S.A.	2·2	0·0	3·5	1·3	1·1

While in 1945 the USSR took practically all Bulgaria's exports and accounted for four-fifths of her imports (both of which were, during that year, very much lower than before the war), the Soviet share had by 1947 declined considerably, i.e. to 52·4 and 60·4 per cent respectively. The share of the Eastern European countries (Czechoslovakia, Hungary, Poland, Roumania, Yugoslavia) had, on the other hand, increased from 17 per cent of Bulgaria's total exports in 1946 to 33·7 per cent in 1947. On the import side the increase was from 8·8 to 26·9

[1] League of Nations, *International Trade Statistics* (1938) p. 55.
[2] *Sources:* ECE Report (see Table XVI for 1938 figures). 'Die Aussenwirtschaft Bulgarians seit Kriegsende' by Dr Georg P. Steptschitsch, in *Aussenwirtschaft* (June 1948) pp. 120, 122; *Bulletin Mensuel de la Direction Générale de la Statistique* (Sofia) no. 1 (1947) p. 29; no. 1 (1948) p. 23; no. 6 (1948) p. 115.

per cent. In the first half of 1948 there was a 20 per cent falling off in Bulgaria's exports to the USSR (to 41·5 per cent of the total) and a very slight decrease in her imports from Russia (to 58·9 per cent). Trade with Eastern Europe remained roughly on the same level, with Yugoslavia accounting for approximately one-third of it.[1] As will be seen later, it was intended to increase the total trade turnover with the USSR for 1949 by 20 per cent compared with 1948. Thus the bulk of Bulgaria's foreign trade is still directed towards the East, though within that orbit a change has occurred in favour of the Eastern European countries at the expense of the USSR. Nevertheless, a desire to trade with other countries as well was expressed, for example, by Mr Kolarov, then provisional President of the Republic, on 20 April 1947: 'Our Government has a policy which favours trade with all countries. We have concluded, and are about to conclude, trade agreements with nearly all the countries which are of interest to us; in the first place, of course, with the Soviet Union, because when we were in a most difficult situation she rendered us help and gave us all that was necessary in order to sustain our industry and our economy. In future too she will occupy a prominent place in our foreign trade relations. However, we also desire to trade with all other countries, in so far as such trading is commercially advantageous and fits in with our policy of national independence.'[2]

In 1947 Bulgaria again traded with over twenty countries, and has since extended her trade to a few more. But trade with the United States and Great Britain is diminishing. This is attributed in a Soviet article[3] to the 'unfriendly policy of the Governments of those countries towards the countries of the People's Democracy'. Great Britain's share in 1947 and the first quarter of 1948 did not exceed 0·5 per cent of both Bulgaria's imports and exports (respectively 7·1 per cent and 4·8 per cent in 1938). The United States' share in the first quarter of 1948 was 1·2 per cent of total imports and 0·3 of exports (respectively 2·7 per cent and 3·4 per cent in 1938).

Immediately after the war, not only the direction of trade but also the range of goods changed. Exceptional droughts in

---

[1] Later trade statistics (analysed by countries) were not available from Bulgarian sources. See p. 97 for the total share of the USSR and the Eastern European countries for 1948.

[2] *Vneshnaya Torgovlya*, no. 5 (1947) pp. 10, 11.

[3] ibid. no. 8 (1948) pp. 4, 5.

1945–6 had made it necessary to import foodstuffs which before the war were one of Bulgaria's chief export items. This, however, was a temporary measure and the import of foodstuffs has since declined. In 1947 the emphasis was on importing metals and metal products (20·9 per cent of the total), textiles (15·9 per cent), machines and equipment (14·1 per cent), oil, chemicals, and transport goods. Bulgaria's chief export in 1947 was tobacco (80·5 per cent of total), supplemented by minerals. The share of agricultural products was, owing to bad harvests, even less than in 1946 (only 3·3 per cent). The export of attar of roses too had declined from 3·0 in 1936 to 0·9 per cent; that of wines and spirits from 6·5 to 1·2 per cent.[1]

To speed up the recovery and development of the country's economy, the Bulgarian Supreme Economic Council adopted a two-year plan in January 1947 which aimed at an increase of agricultural production in 1948 of 34 per cent compared with pre-war years, and in industry at an over-all increase of 67 per cent. Thus Bulgaria, still a predominantly agricultural country with relatively primitive methods of cultivation, is to develop rapidly her hitherto insignificant industry.

The number of industrial workers was to be increased by 16 per cent (compared with 1946); productivity of labour by 15 and 20 per cent according to industries. Goods traffic by rail should increase by 34 per cent, by road 80 per cent, by waterways 130 per cent.

With regard to foreign trade, the two-year plan foresaw a considerable increase. Calculated in 1946 prices, exports in 1948 were to exceed those of 1946 by 148 per cent; the increase was to be obtained by exporting more tobacco, attar of roses, fruit, livestock, poultry and game, eggs, beans, cement, and coal. The 1948 imports were planned at 146 per cent above those of 1946, covering chiefly machines, tractors, transport goods and other equipment, ferrous and non-ferrous metals, fertilizers, and chemicals, goods required for the industrialization of the country and the mechanization and intensification of its agriculture.[2]

A five-year plan was adopted for the period 1949–53. It aims at the 'utmost development of heavy industry' and mechanization of agriculture.[3] As far as trade is concerned, the plan will ob-

[1] ibid. no. 8 (1948) p. 2.
[2] ibid. no. 5 (1947) pp. 7–10; no. 8 (1948) p. 3.
[3] *Soviet Monitor* (30 December 1948).

viously necessitate greater imports of industrial and agricultural machinery and industrial raw materials, which Bulgaria apparently endeavours to obtain partly from the USSR, partly from Czechoslovakia and Poland, and, until recently, Yugoslavia.

The adoption of the first national economic plan was preceded and accompanied by the nationalization of key industries, banking and mining, an agrarian reform, the setting up of co-operative farms, and the reorganization of international and foreign trade. Export and import trade was virtually nationalized: Government and semi-Government concerns were set up under the general supervision and direction of the Ministry of Trade. These export and import concerns negotiate details of trade agreements with foreign firms within the framework of a general trade agreement, or they conclude individual contracts where no general agreements exist.

Trade Agreements with the USSR

The first large-scale post-war economic agreement with the USSR was concluded on 14 March 1945, under which Bulgaria 'received goods vital for her economy' (Dr Stepschitsch), at prices which do not, however, appear to have been very favourable to Bulgaria.[1] It is understood, for example, that in 1945, 5,000 kilogrammes of attar of roses were sold to the USSR at a total price of 550 million leva, i.e. at only $386 per kg. calculated at the official rate of exchange of 285 leva to the dollar. Calculated at the free exchange rate of about 1,000 leva to the dollar, the price equalled only $110 per kg., whereas the world market price at that time was about $1,200 per kg. In re-selling the oil, the USSR thereby cashed a considerable profit.

No details were available as to the volume and nature of goods under this agreement, but Soviet deliveries up to October 1945 were reported as having included 80,000 tons of oil products, 19,000 tons of metals, 3 million litres of mineral oils, 6,000 tons of cotton, 1,800 tons of wool, 3,800 tons of paper, 3,500 tons of rubber, 150 trucks, 80,000 tyres, 550 tons of hemp, 3,500 tons of iron.[2] Soviet imports seem to have consisted chiefly of tobacco and wine.

---

[1] This agreement also provided for the exemption from stamp duties on all contracts concluded between the two countries and the exemption from the turn-over tax for Bulgarian import organizations which draw no profits as importers. *Financial News* (21 August 1945).

[2] *Neue Züricher Zeitung* (21 November 1945).

Towards the end of 1945 the USSR offered a loan, until April 1947, of considerable amounts of wheat and maize,[1] in view of Bulgaria's depleted stocks of grain and fodder and her extremely difficult economic situation.

It was later reported by the *New York Times*[2] that the loan of 50,000 tons of cereals was to be entered as a trading account in the agreement of 1945, thus freeing Bulgaria from her obligation to repay it in kind, enabling her to improve trade with other countries. Simultaneously the *New York Times* reported that, as from June 1946, Bulgarian spinning mills had ceased to work exclusively for the USSR and were able to begin to meet domestic needs, the procedure hitherto having been that the Soviet Union supplied the raw cotton, which Bulgaria then re-exported to the USSR after spinning.

In March 1946 a second Bulgarian trade delegation went to Moscow and on 27 April 1946 an agreement for the 'mutual shipment of goods' for 1946–7 was concluded.[3] Exports to the USSR for the whole of 1946 consisted of tobacco (presumably largely for re-export), sugar, and other food (classed as *denrées coloniales*) accounting for 74 per cent of all exports to the Soviet Union, fruit and vegetables 8·8 per cent, alcohol, wine 8·8 per cent, metals and metal products 4·8 per cent. Imports from the USSR included: metals and metal products 23·2 per cent of total, textiles 17·6 per cent, resins, gums, mineral oils, glues 12 per cent, medicines, musical instruments, equipment, arms 12 per cent, cereals 11·8 per cent, pulp and paper 6 per cent, caoutchouc 4·8 per cent, chemicals 4·4 per cent, wagons, motor cars 1·8 per cent.[4] The purchase from the USSR of 5,936 railway wagons and 127 locomotives, already in use on Bulgarian railways, did not apparently form part of the 1946 trade agreement, since it required the voting by the National Assembly of a special credit of 2 milliard leva.[5] This rolling stock was probably Bulgarian property requisitioned by Soviet occupation troops and now re-sold to the Bulgarian Government.

---

[1] The *New York Times* of December 1945 speaks of 20 million kilograms of wheat and 30 million kilograms of corn. *Neue Züricher Zeitung* of 17 December 1945 mentions 20 million kilograms of wheat and 100 million kilograms of maize.

[2] 10 June 1946.   [3] *Soviet Monitor* (28 April 1946).

[4] *Statistique du Commerce Extérieur*, published by Direction Générale de la Statistique (Sofia, 1948).

[5] *Tägliche Rundschau* (7 February 1947).

A third trade agreement valid until 31 December 1948 (and, if not denounced, automatically to remain in force) was concluded on 5 July 1947.[1] It covered imports to the value of about $46 million, and exports to the value of about $41 million, the difference of $5 million to be covered by a credit from the USSR repayable over a period of seven years.[2]

Bulgaria was to import chiefly cotton, rubber, 1,000 railway wagons, motor cars, lorries, tractors, spare parts, machinery, medicines, 10,000 tons of fertilizer, oil and oil products, metals, paper cellulose. Bulgarian supplies to Russia were to consist chiefly of tobacco (20,000 tons valued at £9 million and representing over 88 per cent of her total exports to the USSR, which the latter probably bought for re-export), ores, and agricultural products. From the point of view of prices this agreement was said to be far more advantageous than the previous ones. Article 2 of the agreement[3] stipulated that prices would be fixed in U.S. dollars on the basis of world prices on the day of the conclusion of contracts.

On 23 August 1947 an agreement for the delivery of industrial equipment to Bulgaria on credit was signed in Moscow. The Soviet Union agreed to supply equipment for a mineral fertilizer plant, a power station, and an installation for the partial coking of coal, and to render technical assistance in the installation of these plants.[4] According to the *Bulgarian News Sheet* (October 1948) this credit will amount to $5 million.

A treaty of friendship, co-operation, and mutual assistance between the USSR and the Bulgarian People's Republic was signed in Moscow on 18 March 1948 for a period of twenty years, Article V of which stipulates: 'The High Contracting Powers declare that they will develop and consolidate economic and cultural connexions between the two States in a spirit of friendship and co-operation . . .'[5]

On 5 April 1948 the *Soviet News* announced that negotiations between the Minister of Foreign Trade of the USSR and a Bulgarian trade delegation were consummated on 1 April by the signing of a treaty on trade and navigation and of an

---

[1] *Vneshnaya Torgovlya*, no. 10 (1947) pp. 30–1.
[2] *Daily Telegraph* and *Daily Worker* (14 July 1947). (Figures quoted in sterling converted into dollars at the rate of $4 to £1).
[3] *Vneshnaya Torgovlya*, no. 10 (1947) pp. 30, 31.
[4] *Soviet Monitor; New York Herald Tribune* (2 September 1947).
[5] *Soviet Monitor* (19 March 1948) and *Vedomosti*, no. 6 (1949).

agreement on mutual deliveries of commodities for 1948.[1]

The treaty of trade and navigation includes the most-favoured-nation clause. An agreement on mutual deliveries of commodities, concluded simultaneously, defines the volume of and procedure for the exchange of commodities in 1948. It was presumably signed in implementation of the July 1947 agreement. No doubt the latter agreement must have included grain deliveries from the USSR, since it was reported[2] that 'the first shipload of the 75,000 tons of cereals which the USSR agreed to sell to Bulgaria' was on its way.

In November 1948 a Bulgarian trade delegation once more went to Moscow and on 18 January 1949 a protocol was signed on the mutual deliveries of goods for that year. The total trade turnover between Bulgaria and the USSR was to increase by 20 per cent as compared with 1948, not counting the value of equipment supplied on credit. Bulgaria was to receive oil products, cotton, ferrous and non-ferrous metals, machine-tools, tractors, motor vehicles, artificial fertilizers, etc., against tobacco, lead and zinc concentrates, copper ore, cement, and other goods.[3]

With regard to general economic relations between the two countries, other than commercial, the Soviet Government, on 23 July 1948, stated that in compliance with Bulgaria's request it had reduced its claim to German assets from $9 to $4·5 million. The Soviet Union, moreover, promised to remit 2,970,000 leva (approximately $10,500 if calculated at the present rate of exchange given by the International Monetary Fund) paid by Bulgaria for damage to German properties in Bulgaria, and to hand over to the Government, at half the value, Soviet properties on Bulgarian soil, such as commercial and transport undertakings, a credit institution, some land, etc.,[4] acquired by the USSR as German assets after the war. This concession on the part of the USSR presumably was made chiefly for political reasons, and indicates the extent of Russia's concealed reparation claims and economic exploitation of Bulgaria.

As to joint companies, such as were set up in other countries, it has not been possible to ascertain whether they exist in

[1] *Vneshnaya Torgovlya*, no. 7 (1948), p. 20.
[2] *New York Times* (20 January 1948).
[3] *Soviet News* (19 January 1949).
[4] *New York Times* (24 July 1948).

Bulgaria. It was reported in 1946[1] that a Bill was submitted to the Bulgarian National Assembly for the formation of a Soviet-Bulgarian mining company to work under Soviet engineers. Nothing more has been heard since of joint companies, until *Free Bulgaria* reported on 15 August 1949 the setting up of a Bulgaro-Soviet Company for Civil Aviation (Tabso) in accordance with an agreement 'lately concluded' between Bulgaria and the USSR.

In the course of 1949 Bulgaria discontinued her trade with Yugoslavia, which for the first six months of 1946 constituted roughly 7·2 per cent of Bulgaria's total exports and 2·2 per cent of her imports. It is difficult to say whether the gap will now be filled by the Eastern countries or by the West. There is no doubt that Bulgaria needs machinery and equipment for the development of her industry and agriculture, but at present she offers to the West little more in return than tomato purée, grapes, and wine.

---

[1] *Tagesspiegel* (Berlin, 30 March 1946).

Chapter Five

HUNGARY

HUNGARY signed a Tripartite Pact with Germany and Italy in September 1940. On 27 June 1941, a few days after Germany's attack on Russia, Hungary too declared war on the USSR, but war did not actually reach Hungary until 1944. In March of that year the Germans occupied the country. In October the Soviet Army crossed the Hungarian frontier. A provisional Hungarian Government was set up which in December broke off relations with Germany and in turn declared war on her. An armistice with the USSR, the United Kingdom, and the United States was signed on 20 January 1945 and the Peace Treaty in Paris on 10 February 1947.

During the early stages of the war Hungary's economy prospered, being geared to the needs of the German military machine; the country had also gained territories under the two Vienna Awards. Even before the Second World War Hungary, while continuing to remain a chiefly agricultural country, possessed an appreciable engineering, as well as various processing, industries. During the war she greatly expanded her heavy industry (iron and steel, electrical, chemical industries, etc.). This was done at the expense of the production of consumer goods, but total output rose by as much as 28 per cent. Foreign trade turnover increased considerably; the chief partners were Germany and Italy, together accounting for over 72 per cent of Hungary's exports and over 70 per cent of her imports.

The effect of the war and the collapse of the German market were all the more disastrous for Hungary's economy. During their flight westwards the Hungarians, and to a lesser degree the retreating German Army, dismantled and removed equipment, machinery, industrial and agricultural stocks, means of transport, and livestock. In addition the country suffered from Allied bombing and actual fighting. During that year industrial capacity was reduced by about 30 to 40 per cent below the 1944 level (or some 20 per cent below that of 1938). The loss of their reserves of raw materials was estimated at 50 per cent. Hungary's agricultural production was reduced by about one-third. The Soviet Army, under the terms of the armistice, removed more equipment and machinery. In addition, Hungary had to pay reparations and meet the costs of the occupation army.

ECONOMIC STRUCTURE

To cope with the disastrous situation, aggravated by inflation on an astronomical scale, the Government began early to take steps towards the reorganization of the entire economy of the country. A land reform was carried out in March 1945. An entirely new currency (forints instead of pengös) was introduced in August 1946. Various decrees passed in 1946–8 nationalized most of the coal mines, power stations, heavy industry, and food-processing enterprises. Today 87 per cent of all industry is under State control.[1] The main banks were nationalized in 1947 and in 1948 all enterprises employing more than 100 people were brought under State ownership.

In June 1947 a three-year plan was adopted which aimed at the economic and cultural recovery of the country. Industry during the second year (1948–9) of the plan was to reach the 1938 level of production and to increase in the following year by 27 per cent. Of the total investment of 6,585 million forints 30·4 per cent were to be directed to agriculture and the improvement of the standard of life of the rural population; 26·5 per cent to industry and mining; 25·4 per cent to the improvement of communications and postal services; 17·7 per cent to building, and social and cultural work.[2] The working out and the execution of the plan is in the hands of a Council for Planned Economy and a National Planning Office which, in collaboration with the ministries concerned, control the twenty-nine industrial directorates in charge of production.[3] A draft for a five-year plan is now under discussion. It will allocate 48·5 per cent out of the total planned investment of £730 million to industry (with priority for heavy industry and

[1] Railways, postal services, shipping, some steel mills, machine-producing factories, some agricultural lands and forests were already State owned before the war.
[2] *International Labour Review*, no. 6 (1948) p. 633, and no. 1 (1948) p. 54; 'The Hungarian Three Year Plan', published by *Hungarian Bulletin* (Budapest, undated).
[3] 'Further Economic Organization in Hungary', *Industry and Labour*, no. 1 (1949) pp. 12, 13.

E

engineering), 17·1 per cent each to agriculture and transport, 10 per cent to social and cultural services, and 7·3 per cent to housing.[1]

In the field of foreign trade the Government began to act immediately after the end of the war by imposing strict controls over all transactions. In spring 1945 the export of bread grains, and other foodstuffs was prohibited, and in October 1945 a Joint Commission for Foreign Trade was appointed to try to impose—rather unsuccessfully—compliance with foreign trade decrees. The resumption of trade was, however, hampered by a multiplicity of factors (political changes in Europe, Hungary's status as an ex-enemy country, her liability to pay reparations and occupation costs, and the enormous inflation). Since, however, it was absolutely essential for Hungary's industry to obtain raw materials and equipment from abroad, the Government did everything it could to export those crops and luxury foodstuffs that could be spared. Efforts were made to insulate foreign transactions against the effects of internal monetary crises; barter agreements were concluded with a number of European States, in the first place with the USSR. A Hungarian-Soviet Chamber of Commerce was formed and Hungary re-admitted to the International Chamber of Commerce. Nevertheless, her foreign trade during 1946 was less than 14 per cent of its pre-war value (the total turnover in 1937 was 1,071 million pengös).

CHANGES IN FOREIGN TRADE

Before the war Germany was Hungary's chief trading partner; together with Austria she accounted in 1938 for 46·4 per cent of Hungarian total exports and about 42 per cent of imports. Germany took most of Hungary's raw materials and agricultural products, herself supplying industrial goods. The share of the Eastern European countries, excluding the USSR, was 13·6 and 23·8 per cent respectively.

After the war the direction of trade changed completely. Owing not only to the political situation but also to changes in the Hungarian economic structure, the USSR became a predominant partner in her foreign trade. This was not entirely unfavourable to Hungary, since she was anxious to export

[1] *The Five Year Plan in Hungary*, published by Hungarian News and Information Service (London, 1949).

finished goods and industrial products, not sought for by the West, in exchange for raw materials in order to maintain and develop her industry. The movements of Hungary's post-war foreign trade with the countries under discussion will be seen from the following table[1].

HUNGARY'S FOREIGN TRADE

	1938	1945	1946	1947	1948 Jan.–June
TOTAL EXPORTS (in million forints)	3,364	?	420	1,044	792
			PERCENTAGE OF TOTAL		
U.S.S.R.	—	5·2	45·0	15·1	20·5
Czechoslovakia	4·0	64·8	16·0	13·9	9·5
Other East European countries	8·9	6·2	9·3	15·2	13·6 excluding Yugoslavia
			including Yugoslavia		
Yugoslavia	—	—	—	—	10·0
U.K.	8·0	—	3·2	17·0	14·7
U.S.A.	2·7	—	1·8	0·0	1·2 =
TOTAL IMPORTS (in million forints)	2,537	?	370	1,457	1,004
			PERCENTAGE OF TOTAL		
U.S.S.R.	—	25·7	49·1	11·7	17·5
Czechoslovakia	7·0	23·5	10·7	10·0	11·9
Other East European countries	13·7	24·5	9·8	17·3	6·1 excluding Yugoslavia
			including Yugoslavia		
Yugoslavia	—	—	—	—	16·8
U.K.	6	—	—	7·0	14·8
U.S.A.	5	—	19·1*	18·5	3·6

*Obviously including Unrra and U.S. Army surplus deliveries.

In 1945, about two-thirds of all Hungarian exports, such as they were, went to Czechoslovakia, and only a negligible percentage to the USSR; 75 per cent of her imports came from Russia, Czechoslovakia, and the rest of Eastern Europe in about equal shares. In 1946 Russia alone accounted for nearly half of Hungary's exports as well as imports. In 1947 the Soviet share of Hungary's exports dropped to 15·1 per cent, while not quite 30 per cent went to the rest of Eastern Europe. During the same period 11·7 per cent of Hungary's total imports came from Russia and 27·3 per cent from the other Eastern European countries. During the first six months of 1948 the Soviet share had once more increased (from 15·1 to 20·5 per cent of Hun-

[1] Sources: ECE Report, Table XVI; Unrra, OAP, no. 47, Economic Rehabilitation in Hungary (1947) p. 65; International Financial Statistics (August 1949) p. 154; Monthly Bulletin of the National Bank of Hungary (July-August 1948, p. 199 an November-December 1948, p. 278).

garian exports and from 11·7 to 17·5 per cent of her imports). The trade turnover with the other European countries also showed an increase, viz.: from 29·1 to 33·1 per cent on Hungary's export side, and from 27·3 to 34·8 per cent on her import side. Yugoslavia alone accounted for 10 per cent and 16·8 per cent respectively. Thus Hungary's total trade turnover with the Eastern countries, including the USSR, during the first half of 1948 was 53·6 per cent of her exports and 52·3 per cent of her imports. Rough calculations based on incomplete figures given in *Vneshnaya Torgovlya*[1] for the whole of 1948 confirm a trade turnover of approximately 50 per cent with the East. (The table on p. 97 shows a different percentage for 1948.) In 1949 trade with the USSR was to be three times that of 1948. Since Hungary has broken off her trade relations with Yugoslavia (June 1949), the USSR, and perhaps the other Eastern European countries will step into the breach, thus increasing their own share in Hungary's foreign trade. This alone cannot, however, treble Russia's share. Such an increase can only be achieved either by cutting down trade with the West, which seems unlikely in view of Hungary's industrialization plan, or by a general expansion of the country's foreign trade, which is indeed foreseen in the economic plan.

In addition to changes in the direction of trade, its structure has also altered considerably. Owing to the effects of the war, bad harvests, and the initial retarding effects of the land reform, Hungary had to reduce greatly her agricultural exports in the years immediately following the war, as will be seen from the following table[2]:

Exports (*percentage of total*)	1937	August 1946–April 1947
Agricultural products	61·0	45·5
Industrial raw materials	3·0	9·6
Industrial semi-manufactured goods	9·0	17·0
Manufactured goods	27·0	28·0
	100·0	100·0

[1] No. 5 (1949) p. 34. This Soviet analysis gives Hungary's trade in 1947 and 1948 by value for twenty countries (with whom apparently agreements were signed) but excludes the USSR and Yugoslavia.
[2] *Vneshnaya Torgovlya*, no. 11 (1947) pp. 29, 31.

IMPORTS (*percentage of total*)

Agricultural products	31·0	12·5
Industrial raw materials	19·0	52·5
Industrial semi-manufactured goods	23·0	13·5
Manufactured goods	27·0	21·5
	100·0	100·0

This trend will persist in view of the structural changes in the country's economy which are taking place under the impact of the successive economic plans, with their emphasis on industry, as against agriculture. The increased need for raw materials and the growing exports of manufactured goods can be seen from statistics in the *Bulletin of the Hungarian Chamber of Commerce*.[1]

Of the total industrial imports in 1938 the share of raw materials was 41·1 per cent, of semi-manufactures 28·7, and of manufactures 30·2 per cent; in 1948 the respective percentages were: 55·4, 24·9, and 19·7. On the export side raw materials in 1938 constituted 59·6 per cent of total industrial exports, semi-manufactures 9·8, and manufactures 30·6 per cent. In 1948 the share of exported raw materials had fallen to 32·2, that of semi-manufactures and manufactures had risen to 13·7 and 54·1 per cent respectively.

Industrial exports consisted chiefly of heavy industry goods, machine tools, electro-technical and oil products. On the import side the share of finished goods is to be reduced in favour of raw materials, semi-manufactured goods, and other materials necessary for Hungary's industry; combined they are to account for 79 per cent of total imports. The most important items required under this, as well as the new plan, are iron ore, coke, metal scrap, ferro-alloys and ferrous metals, cotton, wool, machine tools, factory equipment, means of transport, and timber. As far as agricultural exports are concerned, which in 1948-9 constituted only 38 per cent of the total, Hungary seems to be concentrating chiefly on livestock and dairy produce, and it is unlikely that the export of grain and flour will be on anything like the pre-war scale.

Changes in the entire economic and political regime in Hungary also necessitated a reorganization of the foreign trade machinery, which is now completely controlled by the Government. Though some private firms still engage in foreign trade, they do so under the control of special State trading companies set up in the course of 1948.[2] These companies, and apparently

[1] Budapest (August 1949) p. 7.
[2] *Vneshnaya Torgovlya*, no. 1 (1949) pp. 31, 32; for list of names see *Board of Trade Journal* (1 January 1949) p. 21.

a few co-operative enterprises, are in charge of all imports and exports of the country under the guidance of the Ministry of Commerce.

ECONOMIC RELATIONS WITH THE USSR

Post-war relations with the USSR show Russia's complete economic domination over Hungary; they have all the attributes of a conquering and expanding power.

The armistice terms[1] signed in Moscow in June 1945 imposed on Hungary reparation payments to the USSR to the value of $200 million, and to Yugoslavia and Czechoslovakia to the value of $100 million. Payment was to be made in goods (machines, equipment, river-craft, grain, livestock, etc.) over a period of six years (this time limit was later extended to eight years and the amount reduced). The bulk of the reparation goods were to be delivered at 1938 prices, which were much below the then prevailing world market prices; the prices for the rest were fixed rather arbitrarily. The result was that after the stabilization of the Hungarian currency in 1946 the average value of the reparation gold dollar equalled about 40 forints instead of 11·7 forints, the official rate of exchange. This obviously increased the actual reparation obligations by nearly 300 per cent. For any delays in payments a fine of 5 per cent per month was to be imposed. In addition the Hungarian Government had to pay the costs of the occupation.[2]

In August 1945 Hungary and the USSR were negotiating a five-year pact of economic co-operation. Its scope, according to press reports, was to be very extensive, since it proposed the establishment of joint Soviet-Hungarian companies for the development of key branches of industry, such as oilfields, refineries, processing plants, companies for the sale of finished oil products, coal, electric power plants, farm products, electrical and other machinery, shipping on the Danube and the river Tisza, air lines, trucks, and motor traffic. A joint bank was

[1] For full text of Armistice terms see the *New York Times* (22 January 1945).
[2] Estimated at 500 to 600 million forints per annum. After the conclusion of the peace treaty a contingent of Soviet troops remained on Hungarian soil, ostensibly for the protection of strategic lines of communication with Austria. By a protocol signed on 29 July 1948 the Soviet Government allocated 44 million forints (out of certain payments by Hungary to Russia to be discussed later) for the maintenance of these troops. According to reliable private information, however, the actual expenditure of the Hungarian Government for these troops was between 60 to 80 million forints per annum.

to be set up to finance trade between the two countries. In addition an agricultural research centre and a 'mechanization centre' were envisaged, to be equipped with all necessary facilities, and arrangements were to be made for the exchange of breeding stock. The project was to be financed on a fifty-fifty basis.

This agreement seems to have been initialled on 27 August 1945 but it was neither signed nor ratified by the Hungarian Government, at that time, since it roused strong criticism and the bitter opposition of the Hungarian business world (not then nationalized), which feared that by the end of the five-year period Hungary's industry would be practically in Soviet hands.[1]

In October 1945 the British and the United States Governments sent notes of protest to the Soviet Government, objecting to such unilateral agreements not only with Hungary, but also with Roumania and Bulgaria.

Moscow rejected these protests. Nevertheless, they seem to have strengthened the opposition in Hungary, since the agreement was modified and finally ratified by the Hungarian Supreme National Council on 21 December 1945.[2]

Simultaneously with the large-scale economic agreement a one-year trade treaty was negotiated and concluded in August 1945. It called for an exchange of goods to the value of $30 million until the end of 1946.[3] The Soviet Union was to supply coke, iron ore, pig iron, base metals and copper, ferro-alloys, raw rubber, heavy petroleum products, tractors and trucks, timber, including pit props and railway sleepers, sugar, salt, and chemicals. In addition the Soviet Union was to deliver 30,000 tons of cotton against which 3,000 tons of yarn and roughly 56 million metres of cotton cloth were to be re-exported to the USSR, representing together 12,500 tons of raw material. The balance of 17,500 tons of raw materials was to remain in the country as payment for the cost of manufacture.[4]

Hungary, on her part, was to deliver 100,000 tons of petroleum and petroleum products, 30,000 tons of cement, 18,000 tons of fodder, jam and pulp, brandy, tomato conserves, vegetables, and certain fine mechanical and industrial instruments, medical instruments, and medicaments. This barter agreement was, in the opinion of the Unrra report on 'Economic Rehabilitation

[1] *News Chronicle* (12 December 1945).   [2] *The Times* (12 January 1946).
[3] Unrra, OAP, no. 47, op. cit. p. 88.
[4] Unrra, OAP, no. 47, ibid. pp. 59, 60.

in Hungary', a framework rather than a cut-and-dried scheme, since it was permissible to change the commodities according to need. Private Hungarian companies were to make direct agreements with the competent State organizations in the Soviet Union. Deliveries were to take place f.o.b. in Danubian or Black Sea ports, or at the Soviet-Hungarian border. Any balance in favour of either partner at the end of the period was to be settled by payment in kind within three months.

The chief aim of this agreement was to secure raw materials and semi-manufactured goods necessary for the rehabilitation of the country's economy and the fulfilment of reparation payments. Since Hungary at that time had no trade relations with other countries the Soviet trade agreement was of great importance. The carrying out of the agreement on the part of Hungary, however, presented considerable difficulties in view of the ever-increasing inflation. 'Hungarian importers', said the Unrra report, 'were unable to fulfil their obligations to the price equalization account; in fact their liability amounted at times (when the pengö slumped badly) to sums which were greater than the whole Hungarian banknote circulation'.[1]

The rapid depreciation of the pengö, and with it the circulating capital of industry, crippled all payments to the price equalization fund, and the proceeds from exports, which should have served as a balancing item, were not forthcoming. This was partly due to the shortage of raw materials, coal and manpower, and partly because prospective exporters were reluctant to sign agreements with their respective Soviet partners, on account both of difficulties of production and of the penalties for unpunctual delivery. After the currency stabilization of

---

[1] 'In December 1945 a special fund was created for price equalization for foreign transactions, under supervision of the Foreign Trade Finance Committee. Importers were to pay into the fund the difference between the nominal rate of exchange specified in the various barter and trade agreements (based on pre-war pengö rates) and the real rate of exchange calculated on the basis of current internal prices; while exporters were to receive a differential payment making up the discrepancy between the nominal price calculated on a pre-war basis and the cost of the goods exported. For instance, the nominal rate of exchange specified in the Soviet-Hungarian Trade Agreement was 5.13 pengös to $1. This means that the importer could obtain goods delivered by the Soviet Union by paying into the Hungarian Central National Bank an amount equal to the dollar price of the commodity multiplied by this rate of exchange. As the dollar in the autumn of 1945 was already quoted at 100,000 pengös by the National Bank the importer obtained the imported material at a fraction of its true value in Hungary and he was compelled to pay the excess into the price equalization fund.' (Unrra, OAP, no. 47, op. cit. pp. 58, 59.)

August 1946 (introducing the forint instead of the pengö) improved economic conditions made it possible for Hungary to speed up her deliveries under the general agreement sufficiently to cover a large proportion of past deficiency, so that by the end of the year trade between Hungary and the USSR was almost balanced, although still far short of the original figure of $30 million.[1]

On 18 April 1946 a Hungarian Government broadcast announced that, as a result of Premier Ferenc Nagy's conferences at Moscow with Marshal Stalin and Mr Molotov, the Soviet Government had granted Hungary a two-years' extension for the payment of reparations.[2] Some prices were rectified and the USSR waived its claim for interest due for late deliveries; she apparently also suggested taking over Hungary's interests in the Petrozsiny-Zsil Valley Colliery Company of Transylvania and reducing the reparations account correspondingly.[3] The full extent of the negotiations is not known but it is probable that other issues, such as territorial adjustments, return of prisoners of war, and problems of navigation were also discussed.

The reparation concessions were preceded by the signing in March and April 1946 of four agreements (presumably supplementary to that of 27 August 1945) for the establishment of the following joint Hungarian-Soviet companies on a fifty-fifty basis[4]: Meszhart (Hungarian-Soviet River Transportation Co.), Maszovlet (Hungarian-Soviet Civil Aviation Co.), Maszovol (Hungarian-Soviet Crude Oil Co.), Malaj (Hungarian-Soviet Petroleum Refining Co.), and a Hungarian-Soviet Bauxite-Aluminium company.

The company with the greatest income is Malaj, from which the USSR in 1948 claimed 9 million forints profit. Maszovlet, in spite of special privileges (exemption from import permits and import duties in respect of fuel, lubricants, equipment, aircraft, or other materials necessary for the operation of the corporation), in 1948 showed a deficit which had to be borne by the Hungarian Government. The largest of the joint companies is the Bauxite company with four to five subsidiary enterprises. Its total value is estimated at 800,000 to 1 million forints, and it is being expanded.

[1] ibid. p. 60. [2] *New York Times* (19 April 1946).
[3] *Board of Trade Journal* (16 November 1946) p. 1628. [4] *Herter Report*, p. 40.

The joint companies enjoy considerable privileges: by a series of decrees published in April 1947 they are exempted from taxes on income, property, transfer of property (including plant, machinery and equipment, offices, warehouses, and dwellings for work-people), rent and lease contracts, mergers, bond issues, and mortgage registrations.[1] A Soviet-Hungarian agreement of December 1947 apparently granted them further facilities.

The Soviet contribution to these joint companies consisted (as in the case of Roumania) chiefly of German and Italian assets acquired both under the Potsdam Agreement and by unilateral action.[2] These companies are administered by a board of directors composed of equal numbers of Soviet and Hungarian citizens.[3] The decisive post of general manager is, however, invariably occupied by a Soviet nominee, who actually runs the company, since board meetings are said to be held, as a rule, once a year only, though quarterly meetings are required by the statutes. The vice-chairman of the company is also a Russian, the chairman and the assistant general manager are Hungarians. If what has recently come to light on the functioning of the Yugoslav-Soviet companies[4] applies equally to Hungary (and Roumania)—and there is every reason to believe that it does—these joint enterprises largely serve the interests of the USSR which, by becoming a partner in them, incurs no risks, but enjoys many privileges. For example, any losses suffered by these companies have to be borne by the non-Soviet Government, whereas the Soviet Government claims advance payment of tax-free profits and dividends long before the balance-sheets are published, based on calculations made by a mixed commission which is invested with extensive powers and whose decisions have the force of law.

Apart from the joint corporations, founded on a fifty-fifty basis, there exist enterprises with over 50 per cent Soviet participation, which are administered by a special Soviet

[1] ibid. p. 41. The granting of these privileges, which were not extended to other United Nations' companies, evoked a note of protest from the British Government in August 1947 (*Manchester Guardian*, 12 August 1947).

[2] A Hungarian decree published in March 1947 listed 201 companies in which Germany had an interest and which were taken over by the Soviet Government which, in addition, demanded full restoration or 100 per cent compensation in respect of war damage to these enterprises. Italian assets amounted to approximately $90 million, mostly in insurance companies.

[3] *Herter Report*, p. 39.   [4] See pp. 90–91.

management commission linked with the Soviet Bank in Hungary. After appropriate amendments in the Hungarian law, they were registered as Soviet-owned property and enjoy extensive exclusivity rights, amounting almost to extraterritoriality. Together with the joint Hungarian-Soviet companies they receive priority treatment in regard to supplies of raw material and fuel, without having to pay foreign currency; they are exempted from taxes and exchange regulations, especially as far as the transfer of dividends is concerned. The Soviet-owned companies have the right to conclude export and import agreements without requiring the consent of the Hungarian Government, and they seem to be exempted from the Hungarian works and employment regulations. Among the most important of these enterprises is a group of twenty-three textile factories, ex-German property, 35 per cent of whose total production was exported to the USSR in spring 1948 at cost price.[1]

In July 1946 the extent of Soviet economic domination over Hungary was already clearly outlined; it caused a further exchange of notes between the Governments of the United States and the USSR, the latter being charged with ruining Hungary's economy. Moscow rejected the accusation as 'completely groundless' and turned down the American proposal for the three big Powers to jointly work out a plan for Hungary's economic rehabilitation, since this, the Soviet note concluded, was a matter within the exclusive competence of the Hungarian Government.[2]

In January 1947 the Soviet Government claimed $200 million as Hungary's debt to the USSR under the Potsdam Agreement which, in fact, amounted to a second reparation payment. The origin of this claim was as follows: Germany had an adverse trade balance with Hungary (which towards the end of the war amounted to RM. 750 million) and was granted a credit through the Hungarian National Bank. The German Government in turn (through the Bank der Deutschen Luft-

---

[1] From private sources. According to these the total value of Soviet interests in Hungary is 5 per cent of her total industrial wealth, estimated in 1947–8 at 150,000 million forints. Calculated at the official rate of exchange Soviet interests thus amount to roughly $600 million which quantitatively may not appear to be very much. It is, however, to be remembered that the USSR controls some of Hungarian key industries and her transport.

[2] *Soviet Monitor* (1 August 1946).

waffe) extended a credit of RM. 600 million to several Hungarian companies for the expansion of their war production (chiefly Messerschmidts) in a safe area, and for the purchase of machinery in Germany. Article 30, paragraph 4, of the Peace Treaty[1] stipulated that Hungary waive all claims against Germany outstanding on 8 May 1945. The USSR, on the other hand, did demand payment of Hungary's debt to Germany and claimed $200 million.

In May 1947 a Hungarian delegation, headed by the Finance Minister, Mr Nyarady (now in exile), flew to Moscow for discussions of this and other far-reaching financial and economic problems. These negotiations, with brief interruptions, lasted until December of that year.

In the meantime a new commercial and navigation treaty[2] was signed in Moscow on 15 July 1947 for an unspecified period of time with a six-months' denunciation period. It was ratified by the President of the Hungarian Republic on 22 November and by the Presidium of the Supreme Soviet in Moscow on 26 December 1947. It was accompanied by a trade and payments agreement concluded on the same day for the period 1 June 1947 to 31 July 1948[3] and was said to provide for a turnover of about $30 million each way. (This agreement was, by special protocol of 2 October 1948[4] extended till 31 December 1949 and is to be valid for another year if not denounced one month before expiry.)

Its conclusion coincided more or less with the beginning of Hungary's three-year economic plan (August 1947–August 1950). It was therefore essential to define imports and exports more specifically than was the case with the 1945 agreement. The USSR was to supply 300,000 tons of iron ore (about one-third of Hungary's needs for heavy industry), 250,000 tons of coke, 60,000 tons of salt (75 per cent of her needs), 2,500 tons of cellulose, 1,000 tons of sugar beet, large quantities of ferro-manganese, ferro-wolfram, ferro-chrome, fertilizers, chemicals, etc. The supply of raw cotton was cut down to 12,000 tons, i.e. to 50 per cent of requirements; the so-called hire-work contract, under which Hungary had to re-export a certain amount of spun or woven cotton to the USSR, was not renewed. It was

---

[1] *Treaties of Peace with Italy, Roumania, Bulgaria, Hungary. and Finland.* (Cmd. 7022, p. 127.)

[2] *Vneshnaya Torgovlya,* no. 1 (1948) p. 29.

[3] ibid. no. 10 (1947) p. 32.   [4] ibid. no. 12 (1948) p. 20.

claimed that on the whole the USSR would supply 90 per cent of the essential raw materials. Hungary's deliveries were to include: mineral oil and products to the value of 75 million forints; agricultural products, such as seeds, legumes, paprika to the value of 60 million forints; cement for 48 million forints; moreover, Hungary was to supply rolled steel, products of the engineering industry, and electrical appliances, 1,000 tons of aluminium ingots, twenty Diesel trains, fifteen electric locomotives, and other equipment, as well as tobacco, alcohol, and cotton goods.[1]

Almost immediately following the commercial treaty, i.e. on 24 July, an agreement was signed in Budapest for the over-all reduction of reparation payments by 50 per cent. Deliveries of metal and agricultural products were reduced by 75 per cent; deliveries of horses and cattle were to stop altogether.[2] Further reparation concessions were made in January and June 1948. On 20 January the Hungarian Government announced that the USSR had granted its request to increase the prices of reparation goods, which would reduce Hungary's commitments by $16,214,000, and to accept reparation goods at Danubian ports, which would considerably reduce Hungary's transport expenditure. The June concessions were explicitly used for Communist and pro-Soviet propaganda, probably in connexion with the European Recovery Programme. The Central Committee of the Hungarian Communist Party in a letter to the Prime Minister Lajos Dinnyes recommended that the Hungarian Government ask the Government of the USSR to reduce reparation payments. An appeal was sent to Mr Molotov, who in a letter transmitted the Soviet Government's consent to reduce its reparation claims by 50 per cent as from 1 July.[3]

The lengthy and difficult negotiations conducted in the meantime by the Soviet Government and the Hungarian Finance Minister, Mr Nyarady, finally led to the conclusion of

[1] *Neue Züricher Zeitung* (22 July 1947); *Volksstimme* (18 July 1947); *Soviet News* (19 July 1947).
[2] *Soviet Monitor* (25 July 1948).
[3] ibid. (6 and 9 June 1948). According to private sources, these concessions on the part of the USSR were linked up with a secret agreement concluded in May or June 1948 by which the Soviet Government demanded that the sums thus saved should be used for rearmament and the construction of strategic roads, airfields, etc. In addition, the Soviet Government was to supply the new Hungarian army with equipment to the value of $10 million on credit. All war production in Hungary was to be standardized and produced according to Soviet blueprints.

an agreement on 9 December 1947,[1] consisting of three un-published protocols. The Soviet Government reduced its claim for $200 million in settlement of German assets and agreed to the payment of a lump sum of $45 million. Of this, $30 million were to be paid to the USSR in forints (at a minimum rate of exchange of 11·74 forints to the dollar) in equal instalments over the period of three years, and were to be reinvested by the USSR in jointly owned and Soviet companies in Hungary,[2] chiefly in the silicate works of the Bauxite Company, of which the Almasfuzito plant is expected to be the biggest aluminium plant in Europe with a yearly capacity of 60,000 tons. The balance of $15 million was to be paid in goods, beginning in 1949 and stretching over four years. The most important items were to be 80–100 new railway engines, as well as railway cars, to be delivered at factory prices. This was a concession on the part of the Soviet negotiators who originally demanded delivery at world market prices which were far less advantageous for Hungary. On the basis of the December agreement the Soviet Government also obtained a bloc of 40 per cent of shares of the Hungarian General Credit Bank (which controlled interests in more than 40 per cent of Hungary's industrial concerns, chiefly heavy industry).[3] This is in addition to the 16 or 18 per cent of shares (originally French owned and later held by the Dresdner Bank) seized as German assets. Other concessions on the part of the Hungarian Government were further facilities for the joint Hungarian-Soviet companies. They undertook, for example, to provide labour and processing for the manufacture of additional goods for the USSR to be delivered at cost price from Soviet-supplied raw materials, whenever a company did not work to capacity. The protocols apparently also covered certain provisions in regard to bauxite exploitation rights,[4] annuities for the Soviet share in the three

---

[1] *Soviet News* (10 December 1947).

[2] According to a protocol signed on 29 July 1948, the first instalment of 117 million forints to be paid by Hungary was to be redistributed by the Soviet Government as follows: 44 million for the maintenance of Soviet troops in Hungary (see p. 62, footnote 2); 10–15 million to be invested in Soviet-owned companies in Hungary; about 40 million to be invested in the Almasfuzito Bauxite plant; 10 million for the Soviet Bank in Hungary; and 1,700,000 forints to be used for the purchase of shares to strengthen Soviet control in enterprises where she had minority interests.

[3] *Daily Telegraph* (30 June 1947).

[4] Bauxite is said to be shipped to Russia (and to Germany) without the Hungarian Government's consent or any agreement on prices.

railways, nationalized in 1932, obtained by the transfer of German property rights,[1] and other questions, such as the postponement of the delivery of 60,000 tons of reparation wheat until such time as Hungary no longer experienced an acute shortage of grain.[2]

Shortly afterwards, on 18 February 1948, Moscow Radio announced the signing of a twenty years' treaty of friendship, co-operation, and mutual assistance between the USSR and Hungary, which contained the usual clause (Article V) concerning 'the further development and consolidation of economic and cultural ties' between the two countries.[3]

After lengthy negotiations the trade agreement which had expired on 31 July 1948, was renewed on 2 October 1948 with validity till the end of 1949. A supplementary protocol for deliveries in 1949 was signed on 18 January. The exchange of goods for the entire period of seventeen months was envisaged at $150 million; calculated for a comparable period of time this meant an increase of over 100 per cent over the 1947–8 trade. The agreement was described by Mr Sandor Ronai, Hungarian Minister of Commerce, as the most important yet concluded, which would fully guarantee Hungary's requirements in regard to raw materials and almost fully satisfy the needs of the medium industry, in particular the textile industry.[4] Soviet deliveries were to include twice the previous quantity of raw cotton (over 50 per cent of Hungary's needs), cellulose (quantity increased by 150 per cent), pig iron (40 per cent increase), iron ore, coke (the last three items will cover about 60 per cent of Hungary's requirements), ferrous metals (50 per cent of requirements), chemical products, such as acetone, resin, phenol, caustic potassium, borax, and others for the textile and leather industry, phosphates, asbestos, copper, nickel.[5] In addition Hungary was to receive from the USSR ball-bearings, drilling machines, machine tools, motor vehicles, and other machinery necessary for the modernization of her industry and agriculture.[6] The assumption[7] that Soviet deliveries would include

[1] *The Times* (13 December 1947); *Manchester Guardian* (20 December 1947); *New York Times* (5 May 1948).
[2] *Neue Züricher Zeitung* (21 December 1947).
[3] *Soviet Monitor* (19 February 1948).
[4] *Soviet News* (14 October 1948); *Die Wirtschaft* (2 January 1949) pp. 64–5.
[5] *Neue Züricher Zeitung* (22 October 1948).
[6] *New York Times* (4 November 1948).
[7] *Observer* (10 October 1948).

equipment for the new Hungarian army and air force could not be verified from Hungarian or Soviet sources.

In return Hungary is to deliver under the agreement both heavy and light industry goods, bauxite, oil, and agricultural products. The most important items are locomotives, railway carriages, Diesel motors, goods and passenger lifts, compressors, refrigerators, ship and electro-motors, and X-ray apparatus. Export to Russia of cotton textiles was expected to increase four-fold, constituting about 40 per cent of Hungary's total cotton textile exports. Agricultural products were to comprise sixfold increased quantities of wine distillates, maize starch, paprika, seed, pigs, and other products.[3] Part of the machinery which the USSR had agreed to take over under the commercial agreement was originally manufactured to Soviet specifications as reparation goods. After the reduction of reparation claims, these machines had become redundant and Hungary would have found it impossible to place them elsewhere.

The trade agreement under discussion seems to have been accompanied by a special long-term agreement for delivery of machines to the USSR to the value of $150 million over a period of five years (1950–4). There is no indication as to whether this is an ordinary barter agreement, with Russian return deliveries to be fixed at a later date, or whether some special financial agreements were made to pay for the machinery in due course.

[3] *Neue Züricher Zeitung* (22 October 1948).

Chapter Six

ROUMANIA

On 28 June 1940, a year before the outbreak of the Russo-German war, the Soviet Union occupied Bessarabia and the northern Bukovina. A year later, General Antonescu declared that Roumania was engaged in a 'holy war' against the USSR for the recovery of Bessarabia. This was the logical outcome of Roumania having in the meantime been converted into a German base; later it became an active war ally of Germany, its armies fighting on various fronts in Russia.

The tide of war having eventually turned, the Red Army crossed the Roumanian frontier into Moldavia on 2 March 1944 and the fighting was now on Roumanian soil. But on 23 August, after the arrest of General Antonescu by King Michael, military operations against the USSR ceased. Roumania withdrew from the war against all the United Nations and broke off relations with Germany. An armistice with the USSR, the United Kingdom, and the United States was concluded on 12 September 1944, whereupon Roumania took an active part in the war against her former German ally. In March 1945 the Government of the National Democratic Front (FND) was replaced by the Soviet-sponsored Government of Dr Petru Groza.

ECONOMIC BREAKDOWN

For more than four years Roumania had been economically part of the German *Wirtschaftsraum*; the main resources of the country and about 85 per cent of her exports were placed at the disposal of the German economy which, in turn, was hardly in a position to satisfy Roumania's import requirements. Consequently, Roumania's economy towards the end of the war was greatly strained, its resources exhausted. But the real breakdown did not come until after the war, when economic difficulties were aggravated by some military damage, a collapse of the transport system, a rapidly rising inflation, and by two consecutive summers of unprecedented drought in 1945 and 1946. The drought, coupled with the effects of a hurriedly carried out land reform, resulted in a catastrophic decrease of wheat output, which by 1947 had sunk to two-thirds of pre-war.

Reparation payments, the high cost of the Soviet occupation troops, and the breakdown in the oil fields (mostly foreign owned) further contributed to the chaotic state of Roumania's economy. Drastic measures were required to put the country on its feet.

New Economic Structure

In June 1947 the Government decreed the setting up of Industrial Offices, for all branches of industry, thus placing private enterprises under State control, without, as yet, nationalizing them.

It also adopted a law putting the sale of land under Government control; the renting of land was made illegal. (No collectivization took place, but the State Administration Reazim, which owned 153,000 hectares of land, had by 1948 set up over 350 State farms and 130 machine-tractor stations.) Various measures to check black marketeering and to increase production were taken. In August a currency reform was introduced stabilizing the lei at 20,000 old to 1 new lei. The rate of exchange was established at 150 lei to the dollar.

Towards the end of 1947 productivity of labour, which in 1946 had fallen to 40 per cent of 1938, had increased to 70 and in the first quarter of 1948 to 85–90 per cent of 1938. Output in 1946 had fallen to 48 per cent of 1938, but had by the middle of 1947 risen to 60·8 per cent. No figure was available for the end of the year.

In December 1947 King Michael was forced to resign and Roumania was declared a People's Republic. On 11 June 1948 the Roumanian Parliament passed a law nationalizing all banks, mining, oil fields, transport, insurance companies, and all other private industries employing over 100 workers. (The nationalization of the oil fields was preceded by a visit in April 1948 of a group of Soviet geologists.) The National Bank of Roumania had already been nationalized on 20 December 1946, and the chief coal mines were placed under State control in 1945.[1]

Roumania was the last of the Eastern European countries to

[1] *Vneshnaya Torgovlya*, no. 12 (1947) pp. 15, 16 and 18; no. 10 (1948) pp. 2, 3. For details of economic organization see *Industry and Labour* (15 March 1949) p. 218–21.

74

introduce planning. It was not until December 1948 that the first one-year economic plan was adopted to raise both industrial and agricultural output and 'to lay the foundations for future economic plans extending over longer periods'. It should be noted that Roumania today is still chiefly an agrarian country, with 76·6 per cent of its population working on the land (census of 1948). It is the intention of the Roumanian Government to modernize and intensify the country's rather backward agriculture by creating large State and co-operative farms, but the primary aim of the plan is the expansion of heavy engineering and the production of capital goods: 47·2 per cent out of a total capital investment of 82 milliard lei will be allocated for this purpose; 21·2 per cent for the improvement of the transport system, and only 9·3 per cent to agriculture and forestry. It is intended to produce machinery and agricultural implements, which so far have had to be imported. In agriculture the greatest increase is foreseen for cotton (580 per cent of 1948), and hemp (204 per cent); the number of pigs is to increase by 120 and that of cattle by 17 per cent over 1948.[1]

A five-year economic plan for 1950-5, is supposed to increase industrial production very considerably: for instance, production of steel by 1955 is to be 1,250,000 tons (as against 100,000 tons before the war), cast iron 1 million tons (against 50,000), coal 8 million tons (against 2 million), coke 700,000 tons (against 70,000), electric power 2 million kw (as against 600,000).[2]

FOREIGN TRADE: ORGANIZATION AND TRENDS

During the first six months of 1948 the Roumanian Government reorganized and restricted the participation of private capital in foreign trade. In February several State companies for foreign trade were set up: Textilimport (for the import of raw materials and the export of manufactured goods), Romano-export (for the export of agricultural products), Exportlemn (for timber), Romcereal (for grain), Petrolexport (for the export of oil and import of chemicals). In July two more companies were established: Metalloimport and Fourage-export. The system of premiums introduced on 15 August 1947 in favour of individual exporters or importers was amended

[1] *Vneshnaya Torgovlya,* no. 3 (1949) pp. 26-7.
[2] *Roumanian News* (11 September 1949).

and it was decided that premiums should henceforth be paid into a pool at the National Bank.

On 13 April 1948 a new Constitution was adopted, on the strength of which all internal and foreign trade was placed under Government control, whether carried out by State, private, or co-operative undertakings. A decree of 6 May 1948 created a Ministry of Trade, which was responsible for the drafting and executing of export and import plans in collaboration with the departments concerned, and the setting up of a system of prices and tariffs. The central administrative organs of the Ministry of Trade are the 'directorates' for the various branches of industry. For example, the directorates for economics and for planning are in charge of the planning of foreign trade; the directorates for exports and imports are each responsible for discovering export surpluses or determining import needs, etc. But it is the 'State' shareholder[1] companies that are immediately concerned with foreign trade. They may be set up by the Ministry of Trade without the sanction of the Council of Ministers for any particular commodity or group of commodities, for example, Alimentexport (for the export of cereals and livestock, set up in August 1948). These companies are provided with capital and their statutes are drafted by the Ministry of Trade. Their management consists of a director-general and two or three directors, all appointed by the Ministry for a period of two years. The companies issue registered shares which are at the disposal of the Ministry of Trade. Dividends are not paid. Profits from foreign or internal transactions go to the Ministry of Finance.[2] A special Ministry of Foreign Trade was set up in October 1948.

The economic plan for 1949 intends to increase the total foreign trade turnover considerably (exports by 37 per cent over those of 1948 and imports by 36 per cent). Before the war[3] Roumania's chief exports were oil, foodstuffs, and timber, which in 1938 constituted 42·7, 28·9, and 11·4 per cent respectively of total exports. Her chief imports were metals, machines, textiles, and yarns, constituting in 1938 28·8, 19·0, and 13·4

[1] In Russian the term *aktsionernoe obshchestvo* is used, the equivalent of the German *Aktiengesellschaft*.
[2] *Vneshnaya Torgovlya*, no. 11 (1948) p. 24 quoting the Roumanian *Monitorul Official*.
[3] League of Nations, *International Trade Statistics 1938*, pp. 226–7 and *Vneshnaya Torgovlya*, no. 12 (1947) p. 15.

per cent of the total. Her chief trading partner was Germany, which together with Austria accounted in 1938 for 27·3 per cent of Roumania's total exports of $154 million and for 37·2 per cent of imports totalling in that year $137 million. The share of Eastern European countries was 18·2 per cent each way. Trade with Russia was negligible.[1]

In 1947 Roumania's total exports amounted to $34·3 million; oil and oil products constituted 28·4 per cent, timber and timber products 25·4 per cent. The export of finished and semi-finished goods had greatly increased compared with pre-war years. On the import side there was a sharp rise of industrial raw materials, equipment, and agricultural machinery. Total imports amounted to $61·3 million, and consisted of: grain and flour 37·7 per cent of total, iron and steel 15·2, cotton 14·3, apparatus and machines 5·3, coke and coal 5·2, transport equipment 4·6, seeds 4·5, chemicals and pharmaceuticals 3 per cent. The share of foodstuffs in Roumania's import had risen from 5 per cent in 1938 to 39·5 per cent; the share of raw materials and semi-manufactured goods from 21·7 to 35·9 per cent. Trade in 1947 was, however, conducted largely with the Eastern area. It is estimated that about 51 per cent of Roumania's exports and 42·3 per cent of her imports were transacted with Russia, the other Eastern European countries accounting for 36·4 and 18·3 per cent respectively. The share of other European countries was 4·9 and 7·2; that of the Near East 3·6 and 2·7, and the share of the United States was 0·6 per cent of Roumania's exports and 20 per cent of her imports.

Trade in 1948 showed total exports to the value of $80 million and imports to the value of $86 million. The respective percentage shares of the various countries were: on the export side: USSR estimated at 18·7 per cent; Eastern Europe 47·5; United Kingdom 15; on the import side: USSR estimated at 34·8 per cent; Eastern Europe 38·3 per cent, United Kingdom 3·5; United States 8·1 per cent.[2]

The composition of export goods in the first quarter of 1948 was: grain 41·6 per cent, oil 14·7, timber 14·5, vegetables 7·1, metals and metal products 3·9, paper 2·9. That of import goods was: textile raw materials 20·3 per cent, machines and

---

[1] League of Nations, *The Network of World Trade* 1942 (Series II, Economic and Financial II A.3) Annex III, p. 163.

[2] The above figures are based on ECE Table XVI and *Vneshnaya Torgovlya*, no 10 (1948) pp. 5–7.

equipment 18·3, iron and iron products 15·4, seed 12·2, means of transport 10·7, coke and coal 4·5 per cent.[1]

RELATIONS WITH THE USSR

Post-war economic relations with the USSR present a complicated and involved picture. As in Hungary, the development proceeded along three different lines: reparations agreements, joint companies for the utilization of the country's industrial resources, and trade agreements. It would appear, however, that the integration of Roumania's economy into that of the USSR has proceeded further and is much more thorough than that of any other Eastern European country up to the present.

Russo-Roumanian economic relations after the war were determined in the first place by the armistice agreement of 12 September 1944. Roumania was to pay to the USSR $300 million in goods (oil products, grain, timber, sea-going and river craft, machinery, and other commodities at 1938 prices)[2] over a period of six years—later extended to eight years. Roumania was also to bear the costs, in money and food, for the maintenance of the Soviet High Command and the Soviet occupation troops.[3] Finally, Roumania was to restore to the USSR all property removed during the war. Under this armistice agreement large-scale removal of industrial equipment, stocks of oil, grain, livestock, etc., by the USSR took place. In addition, the Roumanian petroleum industry was committed to supply annually for six years over 1,700,000 tons of petroleum as part of Roumania's reparation payments, valued at $15 per ton, i.e. about half of the current world prices. The remaining quantities of oil and petroleum products were allocated to the USSR under a commercial treaty concluded on 19 January 1945 for the period of one year.[4]

---

[1] *Vneshnaya Torgovlya*, no. 10 (1948) pp. 6, 7.

[2] See p. 62 on Hungary's reparation payments.

[3] These maintenance costs must have been very considerable, exceeding by far the actual reparation payments. General Nicolae Radescu, Roumanian Prime Minister from December 1944 to February 1946, now in exile in the United States, estimated 'the total value of Soviet extractions—in cash, food, and services—from September 1944 to June 1948 at $1,785 million, i.e. over 86 per cent of Roumania's national income, which, he says, since September 1944 averaged $550 million, (*New York Times*, 18 July 1948); see also *Roumania Under the Soviet Yoke* by Reuben Markham (Meador Publishing Company, Boston, 1949) p. 524.

[4] 'Roumanian Oil', *The World Today* (Royal Institute of International Affairs, January 1949) p. 10.

Next to the armistice agreement, the second step of far-reaching importance for the entire Roumanian industry was the signing of an economic agreement on 8 May 1945. It consisted of several separate pacts and was concluded 'for the strengthening of economic relations between Roumania and the USSR and regulations for trade between the two countries' (without, however, in principle, barring trade with other countries). The most important feature of this treaty was the provision for the establishment of Soviet-Roumanian joint companies for the utilization of Roumanian resources and the speeding up of economic rehabilitation. These Soviet-Roumanian companies were to be established on a fifty-fifty basis, i.e. each side was to contribute equal shares of capital and to enjoy equal rights. In most cases the Soviet contributions consisted of the handing over to these companies of Russia's claims to so-called German assets, or of machinery and equipment earmarked as reparations, but probably found more profitable if left in the country. Only in a few cases did the Soviet Government make a genuine contribution by sending their own goods, such as planes or raw cotton.[1]

The first five joint corporations, set up in 1945 and 1946 under this agreement, were: Sovromtransport, Tars (Soviet-Roumanian Civil Aviation Company); Sovromlemn (Soviet-Roumanian Lumber Company), Sovrombank (for commercial transactions between the two countries), and Sovrompetrol (the latter with a capital of 5,000 million 1939-lei which was to be subscribed in equal shares by the Soviet and the Roumanian Governments). Contrary to the law which stipulates that only companies in which at least 75 per cent of capital is owned by Roumanians qualify for preferential treatment, Sovrompetrol, with only 50 per cent of Roumanian capital, was subsequently granted all the privileges of a Roumanian company, including exemption from various taxes. According to reliable private sources the company has in effect the sole right to buy back State royalties; at auctions of land it has preferential treatment at equal bids; it has the right to export petroleum products in

[1] This is what *Vneshnaya Togrovlya*, no. 10 (1948) p. 3 has to say: 'The share of the Soviet Union in these companies were German assets, which became the property of the USSR in accordance with the decisions of the Potsdam Conference and the Peace Treaty. A large quantity of equipment and machines for the oil and timber industries and transport, sent from the USSR in order to fill the needs of the enterprises of the mixed companies, have assisted in quickly rehabilitating the key branches of industry and transport.'

exchange for foreign-manufactured oil-field equipment. This last right, however, would seem to be rather fictitious, in view of Soviet claims on Roumanian oil both under the reparations and the trade agreements (under the latter 470,000 metric tons were to be delivered in 1948.)

Also in 1946 a delegation from Gosstrakh (Soviet State Insurance Company) visited Roumania to study current problems of insurance companies, and in particular to investigate the position of those with German capital, obviously with a view to claiming them as German assets. The Soviet economic hold over Roumania was further strengthened by the merging in May 1948 of all important banks with Sovrombank which was subsequently converted into the Roumanian State Bank. Several more joint Sovrom companies were set up later; Sovromtractor and Sovromchemicals in November 1948; Sovromgas (for the utilization of natural gases) at the beginning of 1949; Sovrommetal, Sovromcoal, and Sovromconstruction in July 1949. The form of organization is identical with that of the joint Soviet-Hungarian companies described earlier and so, presumably, is the method of administration with all the privileges accruing to these companies and consequently to the USSR.

The actual trade pact, which formed part of the economic agreement of May 1945, was signed for the period of one year, but was subsequently extended till 1 October 1946. Prices agreed upon were stated to be world market prices calculated in lei as the basic currency. The pact was considered to be of the greatest importance for Roumania's rehabilitation. Under it Roumania, during the period 8 May 1945 to 3 August 1947, received goods from the USSR which included the following products (in round figures): 28,200 tons of iron and steel, 12 tons of ball-bearings, 1,100 tons of non-ferrous metals, 70,300 tons of coke and coal, 1,600 tons of asbestos, 11,800 tons of cotton, 930 tons of wool, 160 tons of chloride of potash, 20 tons of phosphorus, 356,000 kilograms of sulphur, 325 tons of rubber and vulcanite, 33,500 metres of transmission belts, 400 tons of electrodes, 1,400 motor trucks, 4,000 tyres and tubes.

During the same period Roumania exported to the USSR 405,000 tons of oil products, 86,000 tons of cement, 1,497,000 metres of textiles, 1,143,000 square metres of window glass, 249,000 cubic metres of timber and other products.[1]

---

[1] *Roumanian Review*, no. 6 (1946) pp. 10, 11.

In September 1945, Dr Petru Groza, Roumania's Prime Minister, went to Moscow and on the 12th of that month another agreement of an economic and political nature was signed which provided, in the first place, for a reduction of Russia's reparation claims. The economic crisis and the disastrous harvest in 1945 made it impossible for Roumania to pay reparations on the scale she had hitherto done (during the first nine months her payments amounted to about 50 per cent of her State budget). Russia, therefore, agreed to a reduction of reparation payments from 1,000 milliard to 600 milliard lei, grain deliveries to the Soviet troops were to cease and delivery of other goods was to be reduced by from 50 to 75 per cent. Moreover, the USSR, in order to ease Roumania's food crisis and probably to strengthen Dr Groza's Government, agreed to give Roumania a loan of 150,000 tons of wheat and 150,000 tons of maize to be repaid in kind plus 5 per cent during 1946–7.

Other points in the September agreement were: repair by the USSR of Roumanian rolling stock and the transfer to Roumania of the administration of the railways; the return to Roumania of twenty-eight warships and twenty-five cargo ships handed over to Russia at the time of the armistice, and a three years' extension for the return of Soviet property (as well as problems of repatriation of prisoners of war).[1]

A second summer of drought and an exceptionally bad harvest prevented Roumania from resuming grain deliveries under the armistice terms or beginning to repay the loan of 300,000 tons. The USSR therefore waived her claim for 100,000 tons of wheat and 44,000 tons of maize due as reparations and in addition agreed to lend Roumania a further 100,000 tons of grain.[2]

In January 1947, a Roumanian delegation left for Moscow to negotiate a long-term agreement. The outcome was a treaty on trade and navigation, signed on 20 February 1947. It was concluded for a period of two years and contained a most-favoured-nation clause both for trade and navigation.[3] As usual in such agreements, it also defined the juridical status of a Soviet economic representation in Roumania and of Rou-

---

[1] *Daily Telegraph*; *New York Herald Tribune* (13 September 1945); *New York Times* (14 September 1945); *The Times* (27 September 1945).

[2] *New York Times* (19 October 1946); *Roumanian News* (13 November 1946).

[3] For further details see *International News* (Bucharest, 25 April 1947); *Vneshnaya Torgovlya*, no. 4 (1947) p. 29.

manian economic agencies on Soviet territory. During negotiations the setting up of a joint Soviet-Roumanian Chamber of Commerce in Bucharest was discussed. A separate agreement provided for the setting up of a joint Soviet-Roumanian Commission to control all joint enterprises.

Simultaneously, an agreement on the exchange of goods and terms of payment for the year 1947 was signed. Russia was to supply raw materials for Roumania's iron, steel, and textile industries as well as equipment and certain types of industrial materials, to the value of $25 million. Deliveries up to a value of $15 million were on a barter basis; Roumania was to supply oil and oil products totalling 250,000 tons, building materials, and other goods such as chemicals, window glass, etc. The remaining $10 million was on credit repayable within four years. Prices were said to have been fixed 'according to international usage and in some cases taking into account the market situation'.[1]

On 12 June 1947 an agreement was signed between the Railway Ministries of the USSR and of Roumania concerning direct railway communications between the two countries.[2] Details are not known, but the press reported at the time that Mr Gheorgiu Dej had been called to Moscow ostensibly to discuss a four-year plan regulating the scope and nature of Roumanian crops, in fact, however, to discuss Moscow's proposal to place a certain amount of money at the disposal of the Roumanian treasury in return for a mortgage on Roumanian railways. Since Roumanian air, sea, and river transport were at that time already under the control of joint Sovrom companies, such a suggestion on the part of the USSR would not seem impossible. In addition Roumania was apparently offered Russian technical guidance in the building of a network of roads and of airfields at indicated points. These press reports, however, could not be verified.

Under the trade agreement for 1947 Soviet deliveries to Roumania were to include: 115,900 tons of coke (representing 166·9 per cent of Roumania's total imports of 1938), 34,800 tons of pig iron (568 per cent of 1938), 119,400 tons of coal (442 per cent of 1938), 95,000 tons of iron ores (83·1 per cent

---

[1] *Soviet Monitor* (21 February 1947); *Roumanian News* (15 March 1947); *International News* (Bucharest, 17 March 1947).
[2] *Soviet News* (21 June 1947).

of 1938). Further deliveries were: 600 lorries, 100,000 bicycles, 500 tons of sugar beet seed, 300 tons of cotton seed, medical supplies, 350 electric motors, 30,000 tons of copper alloys, 74,000 tons of coke, over 10,000 tons of cotton, 230,000 tons of wool, etc.; over 50,000 tons of cereals had already reached Roumania by the beginning of August 1947.[1] Details regarding Roumanian deliveries to the USSR under this agreement are not available.

A new trade agreement for 1948 was signed on 18 February, after the conclusion on 4 February 1948 of a twenty years' treaty of friendship, co-operation, and mutual assistance.[2] Roumania was expected to supply chiefly manufactured goods against raw materials, semi-manufactured goods, machinery and equipment. In particular the Roumanian steel industry was expected to receive 80,000 tons of coke, 25,000 tons of iron ore, 27,000 tons of pig iron, 15,000 tons of semi-finished steels, special steels and ferro-alloys, 11,000 tons of steel ingots.[3] The volume of the trade turnover does not seem to have been disclosed.

The most important development in Soviet-Roumanian economic relations was probably a new revision of Soviet reparation claims which were now cut by 50 per cent. Similar to the Czech request for a Soviet grain loan, the request for a revision of reparations also was staged in an unusual manner and used for propaganda purposes. At the end of May 1948 *Pravda* published a letter from Finland which asked for a reduction of reparation claims, and suggested that Roumania and Hungary might follow suit. Thereupon it was decided at a conference of the Council of Ministers on 4 June, headed by the Prime Minister, Dr Groza, to address a letter to Stalin, which concluded: 'In the knowledge of the feelings of warm friendship for Roumania, entertained by you personally and by the Government headed by you, and of the support given by you to the Roumanian people during the period of hard trials, we permit ourselves to hope that the request of the Government of the Roumanian People's Republic will be taken into consideration.' On 7 June Dr Groza received a personal

[1] *International News* (Bucharest 23 August 1947); *Roumanian News* (19 November 1947; 12 December 1947; 14 November 1948).
[2] *The Times* (6 February 1948); *Vedamasti*, no. 5 (1949)
[3] *Neue Züricher Zeitung* (27 February 1948); *Daily Worker* (20 February 1948); *Roumanian News* (14 November 1948).

message from Stalin agreeing to a reduction of the remaining reparation payments by 50 per cent beginning 1 July. The Roumanian Grand National Assembly and Dr Groza personally sent enthusiastic messages of thanks to Stalin for this 'substantial economic aid' and the proof of friendship and support to peoples 'who are fighting for national independence, democracy, and peace'.[1] It is not known whether special conditions were attached to this reduction, as seems to have been the case with Hungary.

On 1 December, a Roumanian trade delegation headed by the new Foreign Trade Minister, Mr Byrlandeanu, went to Moscow to negotiate a new agreement on trade turnover and payments for 1949, and an agreement on Soviet technical assistance to Roumania; both were signed on 24 January 1949. The value of goods to be exchanged under this agreement was expected to amount to nearly 465 million roubles each way, an increase, according to *Tass Agency*, of 150 per cent compared with 1948. The USSR was to supply industrial equipment, motor vehicles, metals, agricultural machinery, iron ore, coke, cotton seeds, etc., in exchange for oil, timber, locomotives, cars, barges, chemicals, meat products, consumer goods, and other articles.[2]

In giving this survey of Soviet-Roumanian economic and trade relations, it is, of course, realized that many details are missing. The general impression is, however, that Roumania has to an enormous extent been integrated into the Soviet economic sphere. With regard to Roumania's trade with the West her chief free export surplus at present would seem to be grain (all her oil and most of her timber products being committed for delivery to Russia). Since, however, she attaches special conditions to the sale of grain to the West (such as delivery of steel), no substantial trade with Roumania has as yet resulted, at any rate not with Great Britain.

---

[1] *Soviet News* (7, 9, 11 June 1948).
[2] *Soviet Monitor* (27 January 1949); *Vneshnaya Torgovlya*, no. 3 (1949) p. 20.

Chapter Seven

YUGOSLAVIA

YUGOSLAVIA today has, strictly speaking, no longer a place among the Cominform countries. Though up to a few months ago, from a point of view of trade, she still belonged to the Soviet orbit, all economic ties have now been severed[1] and Yugoslavia is struggling for a place in the Western commercial world. Nevertheless, Yugoslavia's economic structure and her political regime are still based on Soviet principles. For all practical intents and purposes therefore she must for the present still be regarded as a country belonging to the East. Her trade relations with the West are merely an expedient, which may, or may not, have more far-reaching political consequences. It has therefore been found appropriate to include Yugoslavia in this study, however scanty the information about her former trade relations with the USSR may be.

During the war Yugoslavia was occupied and divided into zones of influence between Germany, Italy, Hungary, and Bulgaria. Puppet States were set up in Croatia, Serbia, and Montenegro. Very soon after the invasion, however, the resistance movement (Mihailovic's Chetniks and Tito's guerrillas) made itself felt in the country. Tenacious, ceaseless guerrilla fighting, often against heavy odds, flared up, particularly after Russia's entry into the war. This guerrilla movement was recognized, and from the summer of 1943 was given increasing material support by the Allied Governments.

In November 1943 Tito's partisans set up an Executive National Committee of Liberation to act as Provisional Government in opposition to the Cairo Government-in-exile. At its head was Tito, the Commander-in-Chief of the People's Army of Liberation. On 21 December 1944 the Free Yugoslav Radio announced the drafting of a new Federal Constitution which set up six constituent States: Serbia, Croatia, Slovenia, Bosnia and Herzegovina, Montenegro, and Macedonia. On 7 March

---

[1] The USSR and her satellites have, moreover, denounced all treaties of friendship and collaboration with Yugoslavia.

85

1945 a national unity 'Government of Democratic Federative Yugoslavia' was formed, with Marshal Tito as Prime Minister. In January 1946 the monarchy was officially abolished and Yugoslavia proclaimed a federative Republic.

REORGANIZATION OF NATIONAL ECONOMY AND FOREIGN TRADE

After the cessation of hostilities in 1945 Yugoslavia's major economic problems were the import of sufficient food and consumer goods, and the restoration and extension of the transport system. Trade with other countries was resumed. First with the USSR in April 1945, in July with Roumania and Albania, and in 1946 with a number of European countries and the United States.

Simultaneously economic changes were taking place within the country: in August 1945 a redistribution of land took place and on 5 December 1946 a law was passed by the National Assembly nationalizing the whole of industry (except small handicraft), banks, transport, and all means of communication, as well as wholesale trade.

Finally, in May 1946 a law on planning and the setting up of State planning organs was adopted. The plan itself was ratified by the Assembly in April 1947 for the period 1947–51. The total capital investment for the five years was fixed at 278·3 milliard dinars (a new dinar was introduced in May 1945) or $5·57 billion. The value of industrial production (calculated in 1947 prices) is to be almost five times higher in 1951 than in 1939. The share of capital goods in the total production is to rise from 43 per cent in 1938 to 57 in 1951. The tonnage of goods transported is to be 279, taking 1939 as 100. The value of agricultural output is to increase from 63·8 milliard dinars in 1939 to 96·7 milliard dinars in 1951, but the share of agriculture in the national economy will decline from 55 to 36 per cent.[1] These figures indicate the extent and rapid pace of the industrialization of the country as planned.

It has sometimes been said that this plan was too ambitious. It is not within the scope of this study to confirm or disprove these objections. But even a very cursory glance at the plan figures makes it clear that to be successful to any appreciable degree, Yugoslavia will have to import large quantities of

[1] *Vneshnaya Torgovlya*, no. 6 (1947) pp. 11–18.

equipment, especially for her ferrous and non-ferrous metallurgical industries, which are to be expanded very considerably, for her projected new power stations, and for the planned improved transport system. This obviously means a considerable increase in foreign trade, which immediately after the war followed the lines of all other Eastern European countries, initially being directed chiefly towards the USSR and the rest of Eastern Europe.

Before the war, Yugoslav exports consisted largely of agriculture products, timber, and metals (accounting for 46·7, 15·8, and 16·4 per cent respectively of her total exports). Her chief imports were textiles, metals, machines, and chemicals (29·6, 14·2, 19·2, and 5·8 per cent of the total). In 1938 her chief trading partners were Germany and Austria who took 50·8 per cent of her exports and accounted for 37·9 per cent of her imports. The share of Eastern Europe, excluding the USSR, was relatively high: 13·1 per cent of exports and 25·0 of imports. Trade with the USSR was non-existent, or quite negligible. The United Kingdom and the United States accounted respectively for 8·5 and 3·1 per cent of total exports and 4·8 and 6·4 per cent of total imports.[1]

After the war Yugoslavia's trade, the total volume of which in 1945 was only between one-eighth and one-seventh of the pre-war total, rapidly adapted itself to the new situation, and presented the following picture[2]:

	EXPORTS			IMPORTS		
	1945	1947	1948	1945	1947	1948
Total in million dollars	?	94	191	?	148	191
			PERCENTAGE OF TOTAL			
U.S.S.R.	63·6	not available		50·1	not available	
U.S.A.	10·5	5·3	2·1	6·7	20·3*	3·2
U.K.	—	3·2	8·9	—	14·3	5·8
Eastern Europe	6·9	46·8	52·3	29·3	35·8	50·8

* Note: probably including Unrra supplies.

In 1945 the USSR was Yugoslavia's predominant trade partner, but her share began to decline in 1946. During the first nine months of that year Yugoslavia's exports to the USSR were 51·9 per cent and imports from the USSR only 28·7 per cent of the total.[3] No authentic information could be obtained for

[1] Based on ECE Report, Table XVI.
[2] Figures for 1945 taken from *Vneshnaya Torgovlya*, no. 12 (1946) p. 12, those for 1947 and 1948 from ECE Report, Table XVI.
[3] *Herter Report*, p. 13.

the years 1947 and 1948. According to private information it appears, however, that the trade agreement of 1947 was not carried out fully by the Soviet Union and that Yugoslav deliveries were also cut down, and further reductions took place in 1948. It is not known whether this was owing to political reasons, or whether it was merely in line with the general reduction of Soviet trade with Eastern Europe.

In conformity with her generally altered economic structure, Yugoslavia's trade organizations also underwent changes similar to those in the other Eastern European countries.

The Economic Council of Democratic Federative Yugoslavia, formed in the spring of 1945 of representatives of various Ministries (industry, trade, finance, agriculture, forests, mining, communication, public works, and national defence) decreed the setting up of an Administration of Foreign Trade under the Ministry of Trade and Supplies. This Administration was, in January 1946, converted into an independent Ministry of Foreign Trade. In the course of 1946 various export and import organizations were created to work under its supervision, for example: Tehnopromet for machinery, Hempro for chemicals, Jugodrvo for lumber, Jugometal for metals, Jugoelektro for electrical equipment, etc. All these organizations, including the Administration of State Monopolies (created in 1895)[1] have the right to conclude contracts with foreign firms, either within the framework of a general trade agreement, or individually.

The foreign trade corporations are actually foreign trade departments of the corresponding central industrial organizations or boards, called 'general directorates'; these latter can be described as semi-autonomous departments of the Ministry of Industry. While the foreign trade of certain general directorates is in the hands of foreign trade corporations, others are authorized to engage in exports and imports directly; this is particularly the case for the general directorates for cement, leather and rubber, wireless, mining, etc.

The actual foreign trade policy is shaped jointly by the Ministries of Foreign Trade and Industry acting on the principles established by the Federal Planning Committee and under the co-ordinating control of the Federal Economic Council. The two latter organizations work in close co-ordination, both

[1] Yugoslavia, before the war, had State monopolies for salt, matches, and tobacco; railways, some banks and most of the iron and steel industries were State owned.

under the presidency of Dr Boris Kidrič, one of the closest collaborators of Marshal Tito.

TRADE RELATIONS WITH THE USSR 1945-9

Post-war trade relations with the USSR developed initially on friendly lines, similar to those of the other allied Eastern European States: on 13 April 1945, a twenty-year treaty of friendship, mutual aid, and collaboration was signed in Moscow[1] aimed, *inter alia*, at the 'further development and strengthening of economic and cultural relations between the peoples of the two countries.' (This treaty was denounced on 29 September 1949.)

The first trade agreement, of which nothing whatever is known, was apparently signed on the same day. A second agreement was concluded on 8 June 1946. The negotiations which preceded the signing of this agreement were attended by Marshal Stalin and Marshal Tito and seem to have covered a large ground. The Soviet-Yugoslav communiqué stated that 'questions of interest to the two parties were considered and full agreement has been reached on all questions concerning economic co-operation, trade, supply of materials for the Yugoslav Army, and close cultural and political co-operation. The Government of the USSR has agreed to supply the Yugoslav Army with armaments, ammunition, etc., on conditions of long-term credit, and also to assist in the restoration of Yugoslavia's own war industry.'[2]

As far as the trade agreement is concerned no details seem to have been made public. An article in *Vneshnaya Torgovlya*[3] mentions in general terms that during 1946 the USSR supplied Yugoslavia with oil products, non-ferrous metals and products therefrom, ferrous metals, machines and equipment, textiles, and various chemicals. Yugoslavia delivered to Russia ferrous metals, chemicals, fresh and dried fruit, wine, and other goods.

On 23 August 1946 the *Neue Züricher Zeitung* mentioned 'preparatory work to form a Russo-Yugoslav Trading Company'. But nothing was heard of the outcome of these or similar negotiations, except for a hint in a speech by Marshal Tito on 31 March 1947[4] to the effect that 'besides trade treaties and cultural conventions, the Government has concluded also

[1] *Vneshnaya Torgovlya*, nos. 4-5 (1945) p. 9.   [2] *Soviet Monitor* (11 June 1946).
[3] No. 12 (1946) p. 14.   [4] *Herter Report*, p. 41.

treaties on close economic collaboration with the Soviet Union and Albania. In this close economic collaboration are the creation of common institutions, such as an agreement on common Danubian navigation, and an aircraft society with the Soviet Union. Negotiations are being carried on with the Soviet Union for creating other societies . . .'

That the two above-mentioned concerns were indeed set up transpired from the Yugoslav request to the Soviet Government in June 1949[1] that the joint Yugoslav-Soviet companies Justa (for air transport) and Juspad (a river navigation concern) be liquidated.

[*Note.* Some light on the functioning of these two joint companies was thrown, after the severance of all economic ties with the USSR and Eastern Europe, by the Yugoslav delegate to the United Nations General Assembly, Dr Joza Vilfan, in a speech on 7 October 1949, and by an article in *Borba* of 30 October 1949. Founded according to Article 1 of the agreement of 8 June 1946, these companies purported to help 'the reconstruction of Yugoslavia and increase of her productive possibilities'. They were administered and financed on similar lines to the Soviet-Hungarian and Soviet-Roumanian companies; for instance, they had a mixed staff, with a Soviet citizen as managing director. Both Governments were to contribute equal shares of capital (the larger part in fixed capital, the smaller part in money). In actual fact, however, these companies seem to have served the USSR chiefly in gaining control over all air and river communications within the country and with its communications abroad, as well as to extract profits from them. Theoretically, the managing director was responsible to the mixed policy board; but the board of Justa, for example, met once a year only so that, in practice, the Soviet director could run the company as he pleased. With regard to capital contributions, the Soviet share (aeroplanes and other material) was, according to *Borba*, greatly over-valued. For instance, old-type planes LE-2 were valued at 4,511,000 dinars, much above the world market price for this type of machine. When the company, in summer or autumn 1949, was liquidated, the USSR demanded 7 million dinars, to be paid in dollars, for these machines. Yugoslav contributions, on the other hand, were valued below their price; for instance, 71 million dinars for an aerodrome which had cost 1,000 million dinars to build. *Borba* also accused Justa of having taken over all the profitable lines of communication, thus damaging the Yugoslav company Jat, of assuming the right to collect taxes, of overpaying their personnel, levying higher tariffs, etc., all to the detriment of the Yugoslav economy.

Dr Vilfan raised similar accusations with regard to Juspad. It

[1] *The Times* (13 June 1949).

appears that until the end of 1948 the Soviet partner had paid only 9·83 per cent of its share of capital investment, while the Yugoslav Government had already contributed 76·25 per cent. The company, said Dr Vilfan, operated largely in the interest of other countries, and not that of Yugoslavia. While Yugoslavia, for example, paid 0·40 dinars in transportation charges per one net ton kilometre to Juspad, the USSR paid only 0·19 dinars, and other countries 0·28 dinars. Juspad also gave preference to Soviet companies for the tugging of vessels. Thus Yugoslav State river transport in the course of one year moved 39,207 kilometre tons on behalf of Juspad, while Soviet vessels moved 59,037 kilometre tons. The liquidation of the company, however, was carried out in such a way that Yugoslavia assumed the entire deficit, while the Soviet Government withdrew the total of its invested assets.]

On 5 July 1947 an agreement on trade turnover and payments was signed by the USSR and Yugoslavia for a period of two years, to be extended for one year at a time, if not denounced.[1] With regard to payments, Article 5 of the agreement stipulated that special dollar accounts (without interest payment) be opened at the USSR State Bank and the National Bank of the Federative People's Republic of Yugoslavia.

Lists of goods for mutual deliveries between 1 June 1947 and 31 May 1948 were agreed upon; the Soviet Union was to deliver 'cotton, paper, cellulose, oil products, coal and coke, iron and steel and non-ferrous metals, automobiles and tractors and other equipment, fertilizers, and divers goods'. Yugoslavia's supplies were to consist of lead, lead and zinc concentrates, pyrites, copper, tobacco, hemp, plywood, and agricultural goods.[2]

On 25 July 1947 (at the time of the first Marshall aid conference in Paris), a comprehensive agreement was concluded for the delivery by the USSR on credit of 'equipment for the ferrous and non-ferrous metal industries, oil, chemical, and timber industries necessary for Yugoslavia in connexion with the five-year plan for the development of the country's economy'. The Soviet Union also undertook to render Yugoslavia the necessary technical assistance in the designing and assembling of equipment and the training of skilled personnel.[3]

Commenting on the agreement, the *Christian Science Monitor* of 30 July 1947 reported: 'The granting of Soviet credits to

---

[1] *Vneshnaya Torgovlya*, no. 9 (1947) p. 32.   [2] *Soviet News* (30 July 1947).
[3] *Vneshnaya Torgovlya*, op. cit.

Yugoslavia would seem to answer in part the question of how Yugoslavia hopes to carry out the ambitious industrial programme of the five-year plan'. Russia's intended large-scale deliveries are interpreted as signs of recovery of Soviet industry, 'but also of the importance attached by the USSR to assisting its neighbours to offset the loss of American aid under the Marshall Plan'. The *New York Times* of 31 July 1947 commented in a similar way saying that 'Moscow has offset the Marshall Plan with something more than a military and cultural alliance'.

EFFECT OF THE TITO-COMINFORM CONFLICT ON FOREIGN TRADE

However, as a result of the Tito-Cominform dispute, which came into the open in June 1948, relations between the USSR and Yugoslavia immediately became uncertain and strained. This, in turn, affected their trade relations, resulting in a delay in renewing the short-term agreement which had expired on 31 May 1948. It was not till the end of October 1948 that a trade delegation headed by the Yugoslav Minister of Foreign Trade, Mr Popovic, went to Moscow (at precisely the time when another Yugoslav trade delegation was negotiating in London), and remained there for two months. The 'Protocol for the Exchange of Goods for 1949' between the Soviet Union and Yugoslavia was finally signed on 27 December 1948, but it showed drastic cuts in the mutual trade turnover. The Soviet Government, in announcing the agreement, made the following comment: 'In view of the unfriendly policy of the Yugoslav Government towards the Soviet Union, which has made impossible the continuation of large-scale economic co-operation between the USSR and Yugoslavia, the protocol foresees for 1949 a decrease in the goods turnover between these two countries to one-eighth of the 1948 volume'.[1] The Yugoslav Government, on the other hand, announcing this agreement, said the reduction was due to the Yugoslav refusal to accept unfavourable terms, i.e. a Soviet proposal to reduce Yugoslav imports of cotton, crude oil, etc., and to increase Yugoslav exports.

The new agreement provided for the import of Soviet crude-oil products, drilling equipment, and chemicals in exchange

[1] *Pravda* (31 December 1948).

for lead, hemp, tannin, and other materials Yugoslavia's 'liabilities for Soviet services' (presumably the services of Soviet technicians) were to be settled in goods, to be delivered in 1949.[1] From the statement it was not absolutely clear whether in Soviet opinion, the impossibility of economic co-operation referred equally to deliveries on credit of large-scale equipment agreed upon in July 1947. Subsequent events leave, however, no doubt about their suspension. It is also very unlikely that any exchange of goods at all has taken place during 1949, despite the trade protocol signed in December 1948.

Finally, after some months of hesitation, a complete economic boycott was imposed on Yugoslavia. Czechoslovakia suspended all exports to Yugoslavia in June 1949, and Hungary denounced her trade agreement. The Polish Government ordered a complete stoppage of exports in July. Bulgaria and Roumania followed suit.

The Yugoslav Government have succeeded in averting an economic breakdown and disaster by expanding their trade with the Western world. Their turnover with the United States in 1949 was expected to reach the sum of $24 million (about double the 1948 figure). On 8 September 1949 the United States Export and Import Bank granted Yugoslavia a loan of $20 million for the development of her mining industry and the purchase of other goods and services. In October Yugoslavia received a 2·7 million dollar loan from the International Bank for Reconstruction and Development for the purchase of timber equipment. Negotiations with Great Britain led to the conclusion on 26 December 1949 of a five-year trade agreement (total turnover £110 million) and the granting of a long-term credit of £8 million. It may therefore be expected that—whatever hardships lie ahead for the Yugoslav population—economically the country will be able to survive the blockade imposed on her by the USSR and her satellites. The carrying out of her economic plan may be retarded but it is probably now not imperilled. For the Cominform countries the loss of Yugoslavia as a buyer will probably not be too great, since her chief requirements, machines and equipment, are in any case none too abundant in the East. It is a different matter with Yugoslavia as a supplier of valuable metals such as copper, zinc, mercury, antimony, etc., which now find their way to the West. Before the Cominform

[1] *Manchester Guardian* (1 January 1949).

conflict 72 per cent of Yugoslavia's copper and 59 per cent of her lead production went to the USSR and the rest of Eastern Europe. The importance of this loss can be measured by the fury of the Soviet-inspired accusations in the Cominform paper *For a Lasting Peace, for a People's Democracy*, flung against the Tito Government because of his 'sell-out of Yugoslavia's freedom and independence' to the capitalist States. Nevertheless, Tito's economic ties with the West are growing and it remains to be seen how far this will influence the ideological allegiance of Tito and his Government.

Chapter Eight

CONCLUSIONS

SINCE the conclusion of this study, the Research and Planning Division, Economic Commission for Europe of the United Nations, has published its *Economic Survey for Europe in 1948* (Geneva, 1949) which contains comprehensive tables on pre-war and post-war trade in Europe, with a brief analysis in particular of the trade within Eastern Europe (pages 145–7). Summing up the results of the present study, supplemented by the findings of ECE, the following picture emerges.

Before the Second World War trade among the Eastern European countries, including the USSR, was extremely small. It amounted in 1938 to only 2·4 per cent, i.e. $168 million out of a total intra-European trade turnover of $6,912 million. Trade between Eastern and Western Europe in that year amounted to $1,751 million, or 25·3 per cent. After an almost complete economic collapse of the Eastern European countries, immediately after the war, foreign trade in 1946 began to recover, but its direction had changed greatly. In 1947 the total intra-European trade was still only just over half of pre-war, i.e. $3,789 million (calculated in 1938 f.o.b. prices), but trade among the Eastern European countries themselves had risen to 7·4 per cent of the total (to $259 million), whereas that of European East-West trade had fallen to 14·9 per cent ($566 million). In 1948 a further recovery occurred, showing at the same time a further growth of trade within the Eastern area. The respective figures were: total intra-European trade $4,797 million; Eastern trade $483 million (about 10 per cent of total); East-West trade in Europe $731 million, i.e. 15·2 per cent. Thus trade in Eastern Europe, including the USSR, had in 1948 risen to almost three times the value of 1938. Calculated in current f.o.b. dollar prices, the increase is larger still, as will be seen from the following table[1]:

[1] ECE Report, Tables 46, 82, 84.

	TRADE AMONG EASTERN EUROPEAN COUNTRIES, INCLUDING U.S.S.R. ($ million)		TRADE OF EASTERN EUROPE WITH THE U.S.S.R. ($ million)	
	In 1938 prices	In current prices	In 1938 prices	In current prices
1938	168	168	21	21
1947	259	585	172	365
1948*	483	1,104	297	650

* Figures for 1948 are estimates, because of lack of Soviet-Yugoslav trade figures.

The growth of the Soviet share in the trade of Eastern Europe is very considerable—it shows a fourteen-fold increase since 1938—yet it has so far not reached the volume of Germany's pre-war trade with Eastern Europe. Imports of the six Eastern European countries from Germany in 1938 amounted to $236 million, i.e. to 34 per cent of their total intra-European imports, compared with only $169 million (in 1938 prices) of imports from Russia in 1948 (28 per cent of the total). East European exports to Germany in 1938 amounted to $254 million or 28 per cent of total exports to Europe; to Russia in 1948 to $128 million (20 per cent of the total).[1]

The development of Soviet-East European trade since the war and its relation to the 1938 trade can be analysed from the table on page 97. Percentages have been calculated on the basis of ECE Report, Table XVI, except those for 1945 and 1946 which were taken from the present study. Total trade figures for these two years in comparable dollars were not available, and conversion of the respective amounts into dollars is felt not to be accurate enough. Nevertheless, the inclusion of the Soviet and Eastern European percentage shares for these three years is considered useful in order to show the initial predominance of the USSR in the foreign trade of Eastern Europe, and subsequent changes.

As can be seen, the changes in the foreign trade of Eastern European countries with the USSR since the war are not uniform. There was, however, between 1945 and 1948, a marked tendency for exports to the USSR to decline, except in the case of Czechoslovakia. Eastern European exports to the West, on the other hand, had, during the same period, grown and constituted in 1948 roughly between 55 and 65 per cent of the total exports from Czechoslovakia, Hungary, and Poland; and 22 and 34 per cent respectively in the case of Bulgaria and Roumania. In contrast, Eastern European imports from the West had, in

[1] For absolute figures see ECE Report, p. 145 (footnote).

SOVIET TRADE WITH EASTERN EUROPE IN 1938 AND SINCE 1945*

	TOTAL EXPORTS million $ in curr. prices	to USSR	to Eastern Europe	Total East	TOTAL IMPORTS million $ in curr. prices	from USSR	from Eastern Europe	Total East
		PERCENTAGE OF TOTAL				PERCENTAGE OF TOTAL		
BULGARIA								
1938	62	—	11·3	11·3	46	—	17·4	17·4
1945	?	95·2	2·3	97·5	?	79·6	6·8	86·4
1946	?	66·0	17·0	83·0	?	81·9	8·8	90·7
1947	91	48·4	31·8	80·2	72	59·7	30·5	90·2
1948	91	43·9	34·1	78·0	111	63·1	26·1	89·2
				76·0				*82·1*
CZECHOSLOVAKIA								
1938	358	3·3	17·0	20·3	262	1·5	15·7	17·2
1945	?	13·0	?	?	?	32·7	?	?
1946	?	11·9	9·9	21·8	?	9·6	18·1	27·7
1947	567	5·1	14·4	19·5	579	4·3	12·3	16·6
1948	746	16·0	22·3	38·3	695	16·8	20·6	37·4
			38·2					*35·5*
HUNGARY								
1938	148	—	12·9	12·9	116	—	21·5	21·5
1945	?	5·2	71·0	76·2	?	25·7	48·0	73·7
1946	?	45·0	25·3	70·3	?	49·1	20·5	69·6
1947	81	16·0	30·9	46·9	108	13·8	32·4	46·2
1948	140	16·4	28·6	45·0	154	15·5	35·7	50·2
				43·1				*48·5*
POLAND								
1938	223	0·9	7·2	8·1	231	1·3	6·5	7·8
1945	?	93·4	0·7	94·1	?	90·7	—	90·7
1946	?	49·6	6·1	55·7	?	70·3	4·0	74·3
1947	251	27·9	11·1	39·0	393	20·1	6·6	26·7
1948	513	18·9	15·4	34·3	498	22·9	19·4	42·3
				37·1				*41·7*
ROUMANIA								
1938	160	—	17·5	17·5	125	—	21·6	21·6
1945 } 1946 }		not available				not available		
1947	33	51·5	36·4	87·9	71	42·2	18·3	60·5
1948	80	18·8	47·5	66·3	86	34·9	38·3	73·2
				83·9				*63·0*
YUGOSLAVIA								
1938	130	—	13·1	13·1	124	—	25·0	25·0
1945	?	63·6	6·9	70·5	?	50·1	29·3	79·4
1946		not available				not available		
1947	94	n.av.	46·8	?	148	n.av.	35·8	?
1948	191	n.av.	52·2	?	191	n.av.	50·8	?

* It will be noted that in a few instances the percentage calculations for 1947 and 1948, based on the ECE Report, Table XVI, differ slightly from those given in the relevant chapters of this study, which were based, wherever possible, on the original sources. In some cases the trade figures cover only the first six months of 1948, later ones not being available; the ECE figures for 1948 cover the whole year, but they are either provisional or based on estimates. The total 1948 figures in italics, again slightly different, are taken from *Vneshnaya Torgovlya*, no. 10 (1949) p. 6.

1948, fallen off in all cases except in Bulgaria and probably Yugoslavia. This was due no doubt in the first place to cuts in the import of certain foodstuffs and raw materials, indispensable during the post-war rehabilitation period. Yet even with the cuts, imports from the West in 1948 were still greater than, or equal to those from the USSR and the Eastern European countries, i.e. they amounted to roughly 62, 50, and 58 per cent respectively in the case of Czechoslovakia, Hungary, and Poland; only Bulgarian and Roumanian imports came chiefly from the East (89 and 73 per cent of the total).

Within the Eastern area, however, considerable changes took place in 1948. In some instances (Bulgaria, Poland, Roumania, and, probably, Yugoslavia) exports to the USSR diminished in favour of increased exports to the rest of Eastern Europe. In the case of Czechoslovakia exports to both the USSR and the other Eastern European countries increased at the expense of trade with the West. Hungarian exports to the USSR increased very slightly, but they decreased inter-regionally in favour of Western trade. As far as imports were concerned, these—as already pointed out—had generally increased at the expense of Western imports. This refers to both Soviet and inter-regional imports of Czechoslovakia, Hungary, and Poland. In the case of Bulgaria imports from the USSR increased at the expense of those from other Eastern European countries. In the case of Roumania the process was in reverse: considerable increased imports from the Eastern European countries were offset by cuts in imports from both the USSR and the West.

Considerable increases in the trade with the USSR were anticipated for the year 1949 (Bulgaria by 20 per cent over 1948; Czechoslovakia by about 45 per cent; Hungary's trade was 'to be trebled'; Poland, an increase by 35 per cent; Roumania by over 200 per cent). It is difficult, with practically no statistics available from those countries, to predict whether this increase was to take place at the expense of trade with the West, or whether it was to be brought about by a further general expansion of the total foreign trade of Eastern Europe, which at this stage, seems more likely.

[*Note.* While this study was in the press, the Economic Commission for Europe published its *Economic Survey of Europe in 1949.* The following changes in the Eastern European foreign trade are noteworthy: the six Eastern European countries increased their intra-European exports from $1,615 million in 1948 (in current prices) to $1,920 million. The estimated share of the USSR was 20 per cent of Eastern European exports in 1948 and 30 per cent in 1949; on the import side it was 51 per cent in 1948 and 67 in 1949. The Survey gives no figures for individual countries.]

If the execution of the economic plans proceeds satisfactorily, as asserted, production and consequently foreign trade will grow. On the other hand, the expansion of foreign trade, particularly with the West, is itself a necessary pre-requisite for the successful execution of the plans. The chief requirements of the Eastern European countries are machinery, electrical and other equipment, machine tools, raw materials; in agriculture, tractors, implements, draught animals. These needs cannot be satisfied inter-regionally or by trade with the USSR alone; supplies from the East must be supplemented by those from the West. In exchange, these countries in their majority still offer agricultural produce, but in greatly reduced quantities. Owing to exceptionally severe droughts after the war, and the first effects of the hurriedly carried out land reforms, agricultural production has not yet reached the pre-war level. In addition, consumption—also as a result of the land reform—seems to have risen. Consequently, there is less surplus for export. There is also a strong tendency (for example in Hungary and Poland, though probably not in Roumania) to concentrate more on the export of dairy and farm produce, as well as processed food-stuffs, rather than on grain as before the war. The export of timber, chiefly from Poland, has also greatly diminished, partly because of lost timber regions, partly because of her own reconstruction needs. Export surpluses from Czecho-slovakia and to a certain extent from Hungary, consist of heavy and light industry goods, which are of less interest to the West, but which will find ready buyers within the Eastern European countries and the USSR.

Whether, however, trade between East and West will grow, and to what extent, will depend not only on the purely economic advantages to be derived from an exchange of goods, but also on a number of political factors, such as national security considerations, the satisfactory settlement of Western claims for compensation, and the general course of political relations between East and West.

APPENDIXES

1. TRADE AND NAVIGATION TREATY BETWEEN THE USSR AND THE
CZECHOSLOVAK REPUBLIC, SIGNED IN MOSCOW 11 DECEMBER 1947[1]

*(Similar Treaties were signed between the USSR and Bulgaria, Hungary,
and Roumania. Differences in the text of the Articles are indicated in square
brackets)*

The Presidium of the Supreme Soviet of the USSR and the
President of the Czechoslovak Republic, desiring to promote the
further development and consolidation of economic intercourse between the two countries, in accordance with the provisions of the
Treaty of Friendship, Mutual Assistance, and Post-war Co-operation
concluded between the USSR and the Czechoslovak Republic on
12 December 1943, have decided to conclude a Treaty of Trade and
Navigation. . .

Article 1

The contracting parties grant each other most-favoured-nation
treatment in regard to all questions concerning their reciprocal
economic relations.

[In the Treaties with Bulgaria, Hungary, and Roumania, Article
1 says[2]:

'The contracting parties shall reciprocally grant each other most-
favoured-nation treatment in regard to all questions concerned with
trade and navigation and also in regard to industry and other
aspects of economic activity on their territories.'

Article 1 in the Treaty with Bulgaria is preceded by: 'The contracting parties shall in every way develop and strengthen trade
relations between the two countries on the basis of co-operation and
mutual advantage. The Governments of both contracting parties
shall from time to time conclude agreements fixing the extent and
composition of their respective deliveries of goods, both for annual
and for longer periods, and also other provisions to secure continuous
and expanding trade between the two countries in accordance with
the requirements of the development of the national economy of
each of them.']

Article 2

The USSR and the Czechoslovak Republic in particular, grant
each other most-favoured-nation treatment in all matters relating

[1] *Vneshnaya Torgovlya*, no. 6 (1948) p. 26.
[2] ibid, nos. 7, 1 (1948) pp. 20, 29; no. 4 (1947) p. 29.

to customs duties and all kinds of dues and fees; the interpretation of customs tariffs; methods of collecting duties; classification of goods; repayment of duty; re-exports; reloading and storing of goods in warehouses; regulations, formalities, and dues applied to the clearing of goods from the customs.

Products of the soil and industry originating in or transported from the territory of one of the contracting parties and imported into the territory of the other party shall not in any circumstances be subjected to any other or higher duties, taxes or fees, or to any other or more onerous regulations or formalities, than those to which similar products of the soil and industry of any third party are or may hereafter be subject.

Similarly, the products of the soil and industry of either of the contracting parties exported to the territory of the other party shall not in any circumstances be subject to any other or to higher duties, taxes or fees, or to any other or more onerous regulations or formalities, than those to which similar products of the soil and industry exported to any third party are or may hereafter be subject.

All the prerogatives, facilities, privileges, and exemptions which are or may hereafter be granted by the USSR or Czechoslovakia to the products of the soil and industry of any third country, or to exports destined for any third country shall be immediately and gratuitously granted to similar products originating in or transported from, or destined for export to the other contracting party respectively.

Article 3

Neither of the contracting parties shall apply to exports to or imports from the other party any restrictions or prohibitions not applicable to all other countries, with the exception of restrictions and prohibitions applicable without distinction to all countries similarly circumstanced, bearing on public order and State security, the protection of public health, the protection of livestock and plants from disease, harmful insects, or parasites, and the protection of plant seed from degeneration.

Whenever restrictions or prohibitions on imports or exports shall be imposed, each contracting party shall pay attention to the interests of the other party.

[The second paragraph is omitted from the Treaties with Bulgaria, Hungary, and Roumania.

In the Treaty with Roumania the first paragraph is substantially the same, although slightly differently worded. In the Treaty with Hungary, the first paragraph is identical and continues: the safeguarding of works of art, historical and archaeological treasures, and also in regard to gold, silver, coin, paper money, securities, and to goods which on the territory of one of the contracting parties are or may be the object of a State monopoly'.

In the Treaty with Bulgaria the paragraph runs: 'The contracting parties, however, reserve themselves the right regarding State security, public order, protection of health, protection of livestock and seed, safeguarding the retention of works of art, archaeological and historical treasures, to lay down at any time a prohibition or limitation in regard to import or export, should such prohibition or limitations be applied in similar circumstances to any third State.'

The Bulgarian Treaty adds the following Article:

'Until a special veterinary convention is concluded each of the contracting parties shall apply to the import, export, and transit of livestock and livestock products, originating in the territory of the other party, rules and regulations in accordance with its laws.']

Article 4

Products of the soil and industry of either of the contracting parties, if imported into the territory of the other party after transit through a third or several other States, shall not be liable to duties or fees any higher than those to which they would have been liable had they been imported direct from the country of origin.

These stipulations shall also apply to those goods which in the course of being transported shall have been reloaded, repacked or stored in warehouses.

Article 5

In executing the provisions in force for temporary admission into the customs territory of either of the contracting parties, the following objects shall be exempt from duties and fees when imported and exported:

(a) articles intended for the carrying out of tests and experiments, and samples;

(b) machinery and parts of machinery imported for experimental purposes;

(c) goods intended for exhibitions, competitions, and fairs;

(d) instruments and tools for fitters, imported or exported by them, or sent to them before or after they have crossed the frontier;

(e) products of the soil and industry imported for adaptation or repair and intended for export when adapted or repaired;

(f) marked outer packing, imported for the purpose of being filled and also such packing when it has contained imports and which after the lapse of a given time has to be returned;

(g) vans and their equipment, loaded or empty, even if they take up a different load at any place on the return journey, provided that during their temporary stay on the territory of the other contracting party they are not used for internal transport.

[This Article is omitted from the Treaty with Roumania, and is somewhat differently worded in the Treaties with Bulgaria and Hungary.]

Article 6

Internal dues, regardless of the authority on whose behalf they are collected, to which the production, making, distribution, or use of any commodity is or may hereafter be subject on the territory of either of the contracting parties, shall not in any circumstances be levied on the commodities of the other party at a higher rate or by more onerous methods than on local commodities of the same kind, or, if there are no such local commodities, on those of the most-favoured-nation.

Article 7

The vessels of either of the contracting parties, their crews, passengers, and cargoes, shall be granted most-favoured-nation treatment in the ports of the other party in regard to their entry, departure, and stay; loading and unloading; dues and charges of every kind, imposed by and for the use of the State, local authorities, or other institutions or organizations; in regard to the mooring of vessels, the assigning of space for loading and unloading in the ports and roadsteads; the provision of fuel, lubricants, water, and supplies; repairs; the use of pilotage, canals, locks, bridges, signals and lights marking navigable waters; the use of cranes, weights, anchorage grounds, warehouses, wharves, dry docks, and repair shops; and also in regard to the application of regulations and formalities, including sanitary and quarantine formalities, and in general in regard to everything concerning navigation.

All prerogatives, facilities, privileges, and exemptions which are or may hereafter be granted in this respect by either of the contracting parties to any third country shall be immediately and gratuitously extended to the other party.

The provisions of this Article shall not be extended to (*a*) the performance of port services, including pilotage and towing, (*b*) coastal navigation. This term does not refer to the passage of vessels of either of the contracting parties from one port to another in the territory of the other party for the purpose of unloading part or all of its cargo brought from abroad, or for the purpose of taking on board all or part of its cargo from the given place intended for a foreign State.

Article 8

Should a vessel of either of the contracting parties suffer damage or shipwreck on the shores of the other party, the vessel and its cargo shall enjoy the same privileges and exemptions as the laws and regulations of the latter party stipulate for similarly circumstanced vessels of the most-favoured-nation and their cargoes. The captain, crew, and passengers, like the vessel itself and its cargo, shall at all times be granted the help and assistance necessary, in the same degree as vessels of the country providing such help.

It is understood that objects saved from the vessel which has suffered damage or shipwreck shall not be liable to any customs duties, unless these objects are intended for use within the country.

Article 9

The nationality of the vessels of both contracting parties shall be reciprocally recognized by means of documents and licences to be kept on the vessel and issued by the appropriate authorities in accordance with the laws and regulations of the contracting party under whose flag the vessel sails.

Bills of measurement and other technical navigational documents issued or recognized by either of the contracting parties shall be recognized by the other party.

In accordance with this, the vessels of either of the contracting parties, furnished with legally issued measurement certificates, shall be exempt from further measurement in the ports of the other party, and the net capacity of the vessel given in the certificate shall be used as the basis for calculating port charges.

[An additional Article in the Treaty with Bulgaria states: 'Both contracting parties agree further to regulate by means of arrangements between the appropriate organizations of both countries the questions arising from the provisions of this Treaty in regard to commercial navigation.']

Article 10

In regard to the transport on internal railways, highways, and waterways of goods, passengers, and luggage, both contracting parties shall reciprocally grant most-favoured-nation treatment in everything connected with the reception of the cargo to be transported, means and costs of transport, and also the charges arising from the transport of similar cargoes in the same direction and for the same distance.

The provisions of the agreement concluded between the railway authorities of the two contracting parties shall be applied to the transport of goods, passengers, and luggage between the two contracting parties.

[The Treaties with Bulgaria, Hungary, and Roumania omit the second paragraph.

A further Article in the Bulgarian Treaty adds: 'the contracting parties agree that the Ministry of Transport of the USSR and the Ministry of Transport of Bulgaria shall enter into negotiations for the conclusion of an agreement on direct railway communication'.]

Article 11

The two contracting parties reciprocally grant each other the right of unhindered transit for passengers, luggage, and goods across their territory on the same conditions on which transit is granted to other countries.

[Not included in the Treaties with Bulgaria, Hungary, and Roumania.]

Article 12

Since foreign trade is, under Soviet law, a State monopoly, the USSR shall have a trade delegation in Czechoslovakia, the legal position of which is laid down in the provisions of an Annex to this Treaty (p. 107).

Article 13

Czechoslovak juridical and physical persons shall enjoy in regard to their persons and property as favourable a regime as the juridical and physical persons of the most-favoured-nation in carrying out their commercial, industrial, or any other economic activities on Soviet territory on the terms on which such activities are permitted by Soviet legislation.

Soviet State economic organizations and other juridical persons as well as Soviet nationals shall enjoy in regard to their persons and property as favourable a regime as the juridical and physical persons of the most-favoured-nation in carrying out their commercial, industrial, or any other economic activities on the territory of Czechoslovakia on the terms on which such activities are permitted by Czechoslovak legislation.

Juridical and physical persons of either of the contracting parties may sue in court and shall have free access to the courts of the other party. In all circumstances they shall enjoy the same treatment as the juridical and physical persons of the most-favoured-nation.

Article 14

The contracting parties undertake to carry out arbitration awards in the disputes which may arise from commercial dealings engaged in by their nationals, organizations, or institutions, if the settlement of the dispute by a competent arbitration authority formed especially for this purpose, or standing tribunal, was provided for in the contract itself or in a separate agreement drawn up in the same form as required for the contract itself.

Action in respect of an arbitration award made in accordance with the provisions set out in this Article can be refused only in the following instances:

(a) if the arbitration award on the basis of the laws of that country in which it has been promulgated has not received the force of a final decision;

(b) if the arbitration award obliges a party to take action incompatible with the laws of the country in which the terms of the award have to be carried out;

(c) if the arbitration award is inimical to the public order of the country in which the terms of the award have to be carried out.

The regulations concerning the execution of the awards, as well as the execution of the awards, shall be promulgated in accordance

with the legislation of the contracting party which has to give effect
to the award.

Article 15

The provisions of this Treaty shall not extend to the rights and
privileges which are or may hereafter be granted by either of the
contracting parties for the purpose of facilitating frontier traffic with
neighbouring countries within a zone not exceeding 15 kilometres on
either side of the frontier.

[The corresponding Article in the Treaty with Bulgaria continues:
'or to rights and privileges arising from a customs union'.]

Article 16

The contracting parties shall collaborate in the exchange of
technical knowledge by means of visits by specialists, the holding
of industrial, agricultural, and other exhibitions, and also by other
means.

[Omitted from the Treaties with Hungary and Roumania. A
corresponding Article in the Bulgarian Treaty runs: 'The contracting
parties shall collaborate in exchanging experience in the sphere of
industrial and agricultural production by sending specialists, organizing exhibitions, exchanging experimental seed, plants and
parts of plants, and also by other means.']

Article 17

The contracting parties will in the near future open negotiations
for the conclusion of agreements concerning questions of settlement
and the protection of rights in literary and artistic property.

[Omitted from the Treaties with Bulgaria, Hungary, and
Roumania.]

Article 18

The Trade and Navigation Treaty of 25 March 1935 concluded
between the USSR and Czechoslovakia shall cease to be valid on
the day that the present Treaty enters into force. [There is no corresponding Article in the Treaties with Bulgaria, Hungary, and
Roumania.]

Article 19

The present Treaty is subject to ratification and enters into force
on the day ratifications are exchanged, which shall take place in
Prague with the least possible delay.

The present Treaty is for no fixed term, but shall cease to have
validity one year from the day when either of the contracting parties
gives a written declaration of its desire to denounce it.

2. Annex on the Legal Position of the Trade Delegation of the USSR in the Czechoslovak Republic[1]

Article 1

The Trade Delegation of the USSR in the Czechoslovak Republic exercises the following functions:

(a) activities to promote economic relations between the USSR and the Czechoslovak Republic;

(b) representation of Soviet interests in the field of foreign trade;

(c) regulation on behalf of the USSR of trade between the USSR and the Czechoslovak Republic;

(d) the conduct of trade between the USSR and the Czechoslovak Republic.

Article 2

The Delegation is a constituent part of the Soviet Embassy in the Czechoslovak Republic and has its seat in Prague.

The Delegation shall have branches in the towns of Bratislava and Brno. Branches in other towns of the Czechoslovak Republic shall be opened by agreement between the Governments of the USSR and the Czechoslovak Republic.

The Trade Delegate of the USSR in the Czechoslovak Republic and three of his deputies shall form part of the diplomatic personnel and shall enjoy all the rights and privileges attaching to members of diplomatic missions.

In addition to the persons mentioned in the preceding paragraph, employees of the Delegation who are Soviet nationals are not subject to the jurisdiction of Czechoslovakian courts in matters arising from the conditions of their service. In the Czechoslovak Republic they shall be exempt from any personal or material obligation, whether military or civil, and also from the imposition of Czechoslovakian taxes on the income they receive as employees of the Soviet Government.

The premises occupied by the Delegation and its branches enjoy extraterritoriality. The Delegation and its branches have the right to use codes.

Article 3

The Delegation acts on behalf of the Government of the USSR. The Government of the USSR bears responsibility only for those commercial contracts concluded or guaranteed in the Czechoslovak Republic in the name of the Delegation and signed by duly authorized persons.

Responsibility for any kind of commercial contracts whatever, concluded without the guarantee of the Delegation by any Soviet State economic organizations whatever, which enjoy, in accordance

[1] ibid. no. 6 (1948) p. 29.

with Soviet law, the status of independent juridical persons, is borne solely by the organization concerned, and distraint in respect of these contracts can be levied only on their property. Neither the Soviet Government nor its Trade Delegation in the Czechoslovak Republic nor any other Soviet economic organization bears responsibility for such contracts.

[The above article is omitted from the Treaty with Bulgaria.]

Article 4

The Delegation enjoys the privileges and immunities arising from Article 2 of this Annex with the following exceptions:

(a) Disputes referring to commercial contracts concluded or guaranteed on the territory of Czechoslovakia by the Delegation in accordance with the first paragraph of Article 3 of this Annex, are subject, in the absence of a stipulation for an arbitration tribunal or other jurisdiction, to the competence of the Czechoslovak courts and shall be decided in accordance with Czechoslovak law, unless other provision is made in the terms of the contracts or by Czechoslovak law. In this connexion, however, no undertaking is valid which guarantees that actions will lie against the Delegation.

(b) Compulsory distraint in virtue of a final decision which is legally binding against the Delegation in the disputes referred to may be levied, but only in respect of goods and debts due to the Delegation.

Article 5

The Delegation is not subject to the regulations of commercial registration. It will publish in the official gazette of the Czechoslovak Republic the names of the persons furnished with power of attorney on its behalf and also information on the extent of the rights of each of these persons in regard to signing commercial obligations on behalf of the Delegation.

[The Treaties with Hungary and Roumania contain an additional article which reads: 'The Trade Delegation may give its guarantee on contracts concluded between one of the organizations mentioned in paragraph two of Article 3 and any Hungarian (Roumanian) physical or juridical person.']

3. TRADE AND PAYMENTS AGREEMENT BETWEEN THE USSR AND THE BULGARIAN REPUBLIC, SIGNED IN MOSCOW, 5 JULY 1947[1]

The Governments of the USSR and of the Bulgarian Republic, in order to promote trade between the two countries, have agreed:

[1] ibid. no. 10 (1947) p. 30.

APPENDIXES

Article 1

The quantities and kinds of goods to be delivered from the USSR to the Bulgarian Republic and from the Bulgarian Republic to the USSR shall be as agreed upon between the appropriate agencies of both Governments for specific periods of time and shall be fixed in special protocols. Both Governments ensure the delivery of goods according to the said protocols.

Article 2

The Soviet foreign trade organizations on the one hand, and the Bulgarian bodies and persons on the other, shall conclude contracts for the delivery of goods in accordance with the protocols provided for in Article 1. The prices of goods in the said contracts shall be fixed in United States dollars on the basis of the world market prices prevailing on the day the contract is signed.

Article 3

Provided that the rules and regulations in force in both countries concerning the import and export of goods are observed, the Soviet foreign trade organizations on the one hand, and the Bulgarian bodies and persons on the other, may also make contracts for the delivery of goods, according to the terms of this Agreement, apart from the protocols provided for in Article 1.

Article 4

Deliveries of goods under this Agreement shall, in the absence of other stipulations in the contracts concluded in accordance with Articles 2 and 3, be made on terms corresponding to f.o.b. Soviet ports on the Black Sea and Sea of Azov or on the Danube, and f.o.b. Bulgarian ports on the Black Sea or on the Danube.

Article 5

The Soviet Government ensures the provision of vessels for the transport of goods dispatched from the USSR to the Bulgarian Republic under this Agreement. Vessels for 1947 will be provided on the terms set out in the Annex to this Agreement. The terms and methods of providing vessels for 1948 shall be subsequently drawn up by the two parties. [Article 5 is omitted from the Agreemeent with Yugoslavia.[1]]

Article 6

Payment for goods delivered under the present Agreement, and also payments for expenditure incurred in connexion with trade, and other payments which may be agreed upon between the two parties, shall be made in the USSR through the State Bank of the USSR and in the Bulgarian Republic through the Bulgarian National Bank.

[1] ibid. no. 9 (1947) p. 32. (Not given in full, since no longer in force).

For this purpose the said banks shall open for each other special non-interest-bearing accounts in United States dollars and shall immediately report to each other all deposits made into these accounts.

On the receipt of the information, the respective bank shall immediately make payment to the corresponding organizations, institutions, or persons, irrespective of whether the means for such payment are present in the said accounts.

Article 7

The State Bank of the USSR and the Bulgarian National Bank will draw up joint technical accounting methods for transactions under this Agreement. [The Agreement with Yugoslavia has the following additional Article:

'Apart from contracts provided for in Articles 2 and 3 of the present Agreement, the Soviet foreign trade organizations and Yugoslav juridical and physical persons may, with the consent in each separate case of the competent bodies of both Governments, conclude contracts for the delivery of goods outside the framework of the protocols provided for in Article 1. Payment for these goods is to be made in the currency laid down in the contract.

In these cases, payment will be made in accordance with the provisions set forth in such contracts apart from the settlement as set out in Article 5.']

Article 8

The Government of the USSR and the Government of the Bulgarian Republic shall respectively instruct the Soviet Trade Representative in Bulgaria and the Foreign Trade Director-in-Chief of the People's Republic of Bulgaria to check the fulfilment of the present agreement every quarter, and, should it be found necessary, to work out appropriate recommendations in regard to the execution of deliveries and the state of accounts under this Agreement.

Article 9

On the expiration of this Agreement the Soviet State Bank and the Bulgarian National Bank shall continue to receive deposits on the accounts referred to in Article 6, and make payments therefrom in accordance with the provisions of this Agreement on all contracts which shall have been concluded during the time the Agreement was in force.

If it shall be established that, according to the accounts referred to in Article 6, one side is in debt, then that side is obliged within three months from the day when the validity of this Agreement ceases, to liquidate the debt by supplementary deliveries, agreed between the two sides, at the prices for deliveries made in the past year and on the terms of the Agreement. [In the Agreement with Yugoslavia this paragraph reads: 'If, when the payments provided for under the present agreement are finished, there shall remain in the accounts referred to in Article . . . indebtedness by one party, that party is obliged to settle that indebtedness, at its own discretion, either by further deliveries of goods, agreed upon between the two parties, within three months from the day when the final amount of the indebtedness is established, at prices according with Article . . . or by transferring freely convertible currency to the bank selected by the creditor party, or by gold.']

Article 10
This Agreement comes into force on the day of signature and shall remain in effect until 31 December 1948. If, one month before the expiration of the said term, neither side makes a declaration of its wish to denounce the present Agreement, it will remain in force for a further year, and similarly at the end of each subsequent year. [The Yugoslav Agreement was in operation for two years, and was to be continued, unless denounced, at three months' notice.]

4. Trade and Payments Agreement between the USSR and the Hungarian Republic, signed in Moscow, 15 July 1947[1] amended by Protocol 2 October 1948[2]

The Governments of the USSR and of the Hungarian Republic, in order to promote trade between the two countries, have agreed:

Article 1
The exchange of goods between the USSR and the Hungarian Republic in the period from 1 June 1947 to 31 July 1948 shall be carried out according to the attached lists I and II which form an integral part of the present Agreement. The parties may, by mutual consent, make changes and additions to these lists of goods. Both Governments undertake to do everything they can to ensure the proper and punctual delivery of the goods.

Article 2
The Soviet foreign trade organizations on the one hand, and the Hungarian juridical and physical persons on the other, shall conclude contracts for the delivery of goods in accordance with the lists mentioned in Article 1.

Article 3
Provided that the rules and regulations in force in both countries concerning the import and export of goods are observed, the Soviet

[1] ibid. no. 10 (1947) p. 32.
[2] ibid. no. 12 (1948) p. 20; this protocol extended the validity of the Agreement to 31 December 1949.

foreign trade organizations on the one hand and the Hungarian juridical and physical persons on the other, may also make contracts for the delivery of goods in addition to the lists mentioned in Article 1.

Article 4
The prices of goods in the contracts provided for in Articles 2 and 3 shall be fixed in United States dollars.

Article 5 (as amended by Protocol)
Payment for goods due for delivery under the contracts provided for in Articles 2 and 3, as well as payment for the expenditure incurred in connexion with the said exchange of goods, shall be made in the USSR through the Soviet State Bank, and in the Hungarian Republic through the Hungarian National Bank. For this purpose the said banks shall open non-interest bearing accounts for each other in United States dollars, to be called, 'Account for the exchange of goods between the USSR and Hungary 1947', and shall without delay enter all payments on these accounts, immediately informing each other of all deposits made into these accounts. All transactions on the accounts shall be made by both banks without charge.

On receipt of the said information the relevant bank shall immediately make payment to the appropriate institution or person, having regard in so doing to the provisions of Article 6.

Article 6
The total of all payments on the Soviet side made in the manner laid down in Article 5 of the present Agreement should balance total payments on the Hungarian side and the balance should be drawn at three-monthly intervals while this Agreement is in operation.

In this connexion, however, the balance of the said payments shall not be regarded as disturbed if, at the end of any three-monthly period, the accounts provided for in Article 5 show a balance not exceeding two million United States dollars in favour of either party.

Should the balance of payments be disturbed both Governments shall take steps to rectify the matter immediately.

Article 7
The State Bank of the USSR and the Hungarian National Bank will draw up joint technical accounting methods for transactions under this Agreement.

Article 8
With the permission in each instance of the competent bodies of both Governments, the Soviet foreign trade organizations on the one side, and the Hungarian juridical and physical persons on the other may conclude contracts between themselves for the delivery of goods

apart from those set forth in the lists referred to in Article 1, payment for the goods to be made in accordance with the terms of such contracts, including cases of possible payment in a freely convertible currency, i.e. in a manner different from that laid down in Article 5.

Article 9
(as amended by Protocol)

On the expiration of this Agreement the State Bank of the USSR and the Hungarian National Bank shall continue to accept deposits on the accounts referred to in Article 5 and shall make payments from these accounts, in accordance with the provisions of this Agreement, on all contracts which shall be concluded during its term of operation.

In this connexion, should the accounts referred to in Article 5 show indebtedness by one party, that party is obliged to liquidate the indebtedness within three months from the day when it is finally established, by supplementary deliveries of goods agreed upon between the two parties. If after the said three months the debtor party has not liquidated the deficit by the delivery of goods, it shall be liquidated by the transfer of freely convertible currency to the account of the creditor party at the bank, or by gold.

Conversion of United States dollars into gold or into another freely convertible currency shall be made at rates agreed upon between the State Bank of the USSR and the Hungarian National Bank.

Article 10

The Governments of the USSR and of the Hungarian Republic shall nominate their plenipotentiaries, who shall meet every three months in Moscow and Budapest alternately, to examine the progress of deliveries under this Agreement and also the state of payments, and to draft appropriate recommendations should they be necessary.

The said plenipotentiaries shall draw up model plans for reciprocal deliveries under this Agreement for every three monthly period. The first meeting of the plenipotentiaries shall be held in Budapest within thirty days of the signature of this Agreement.

Article 11

In accordance with Point 3 of the final protocol to the Agreement of 27 August 1945 between the USSR and the Provisional National Government of Hungary on reciprocal deliveries of goods, any balance which may have arisen in favour of either party as shown by the collation of the accounts opened in the Soviet State Bank and the Hungarian National Bank under the said Agreement of 27 August 1945 shall be carried over to the credit of the respective account provided for in Article 5 of the present Agreement.

5. Trade and Payments Agreement between the USSR and the Roumanian Republic, signed in Moscow on 24 January 1949[1]

The Governments of the USSR and the Roumanian Republic, in order to promote trade between the two countries, have agreed:

Article 1

The Government of the USSR assures the delivery to the Roumanian Republic within the period from the signature of this Agreement to 31 December 1949 of the goods agreed upon in list I annexed to the present Agreement.[2]

The Government of the Roumanian Republic assures the delivery to the USSR within the same period of the goods agreed upon in list II annexed to the present Agreement.

Charges and additions may be made in lists I and II by agreement of the two parties.

The Government of the USSR has also agreed to accept from the Government of the Roumanian Republic orders for the equipment specified in list III annexed to the present Agreement; the dates of delivery of this equipment and other terms shall be agreed subsequently.

Article 2

Both Governments agree to take all the necessary steps to develop trade in accordance with this Agreement. The competent bodies in both countries, in accordance with the laws in force therein, shall make decisions concerning the import and export of goods in execution of the present Agreement.

Article 3

The deliveries of goods provided for in Article 1 shall be made on the basis of contracts concluded between the appropriate Soviet foreign trade organizations and the Roumanian foreign trade organizations. Deliveries will be made at prices which shall be fixed in these contracts.

Article 4

Provided that the rules and regulations in force in both countries concerning the import and export of goods are observed, the Soviet foreign trade organizations on the one hand, and the Roumanian foreign trade organizations on the other, may also make contracts for the delivery of goods apart from the lists provided for in Article 1 and, in particular, compensation agreements.

Article 5

Payment for goods delivered under the contracts provided for in Article 3, as well as payments for expenditure incurred in connexion

[1] ibid. no. 3 (1949) p. 20.
[2] Annexes not reproduced in *Vneshnaya Torgovlya*.

with trade, shall be made in the USSR through the State Bank of the USSR and in the Roumanian Republic through the Roumanian State Bank.

For this purpose the State banks shall open for each other special non-interest bearing accounts in roubles and shall immediately report to each other all deposits made.

On the receipt of such information the respective bank shall immediately make payment to the corresponding institutions or persons irrespective of whether the means for such payments are available in the said accounts.

Article 6
The total of all payments by each of the parties should balance each other, and this balance should be drawn at half-yearly intervals while this Agreement is in operation.

In this connexion, however, the balance of the said payments shall not be regarded as disturbed if, at the end of any half-yearly period, the value of the goods delivered by one party shall exceed the value of the goods delivered by the other party by a sum not exceeding 11 million roubles.

Article 7
The State Banks of the USSR and the Roumanian State Bank shall draw up joint technical accounting methods for transactions under this Agreement.

Article 8
The Governments of the USSR and of the Roumanian Republic shall appoint plenipotentiaries who shall meet every six months—in Moscow and Bucharest alternately—to examine the progress of the deliveries of goods under this Agreement and also the state of payments, and, where necessary, to draft appropriate recommendations.

Article 9
Apart from the contracts provided for in Articles 3 and 4 Soviet foreign trade organizations and Roumanian foreign trade organizations may, with the permission in each separate case of the competent bodies of the two Governments, make contracts for the delivery of goods apart from those set forth in the lists referred to in Article 1, payment for these goods to be made in the currency laid down in the contract. In these cases payment shall be made in accordance with the terms laid down in such contracts and not in accordance with the procedure laid down in Article 5.

Article 10
On the expiration of this Agreement, the Soviet State Bank and the State Bank of the Roumanian Republic shall continue to receive

deposits on the accounts referred to in Article 5, and to make payments therefrom on all contracts which shall have been concluded during the period that this Agreement is in force.

If, after the termination of the payments provided for by this Agreement, it shall be established that—according to the accounts referred to in Article 5—one side is in debt, then that side is obliged within three months from the day when the validity of this Agreement ceases to liquidate the debt by supplementary deliveries agreed between the two sides, at prices in accordance with Article 3 of the present Agreement, or by the transfer of freely convertible currency to the bank at the choice of the creditor party, or by gold.

[The Trade and Payments Agreement with Poland and Czechoslovakia have not been published.]

6. Inter-Regional Trade Agreements in the Eastern Area (excluding the USSR)[1]

BULGARIA

With Albania 3 August 1948 for the delivery of agricultural products and industrial goods in exchange for minerals, naphtha, bitumen, chrome ore, and cotton.

With Finland 6 October 1948 to the value of $3 million. Finland to deliver cellulose and paper.

With Czechoslovakia 7 April 1949 for delivery of maize, tobacco, ores, metal concentrates, wines, farm produce, against rolled steel, iron manufactures, machinery, vehicles, chemicals, textiles, glass, paper, some consumer goods.

With Hungary 8 September 1948 for delivery of agricultural products, tobacco, furs, vegetable seeds against machinery equipment, metals, electrical materials, chemicals for agriculture.

With Poland economic agreement 1 September 1948 in force until 31 December 1949. Turnover $20 million. For delivery of tobacco, ores, oil, essences, raw leather, rice, grapes against machinery, tools, electrical and technical equipment, and other industrial products.

CZECHOSLOVAKIA

With Bulgaria: (see above).

With Hungary five-year agreement signed in November 1948. Total turnover about £75 million. The ČSR to supply coke, timber, cellulose, ceramic products, machinery, motor cars,

---

[1] This list does not claim to be complete, since information on inter-regional agreements is not always available.

various raw materials, including iron ore (of which ČSR herself imports 80 per cent from the USSR and Sweden), against foodstuffs (especially meat, lard, fats), aluminium, oil by-products, raw and manufactured chemicals, electro-technical products.

With Poland five-year agreement signed in July 1947 for large scale economic co-operation. A trade agreement was signed at that time to be in force until June 1949 (and since presumably extended) for the delivery of raw materials, cellulose, shoes, machinery, industrial equipment against Polish coal, zinc, dolomite, chemicals, etc.

With Roumania signed in January 1949. One year; trade increased by 35–40 per cent over 1948. ČSR to deliver ceramics, coke, metal products, chemicals against oil products, lead, zinc, timber, bread grains.

HUNGARY

With Albania 14 May 1949 (no details available).

With Bulgaria and Czechoslovakia (see above).

With Finland 25 September 1948 agricultural products and manufactured goods against cellulose, paper and raw materials for the chemical industry.

With Poland an economic co-operation agreement signed on 13 May 1948 was followed by a trade agreement 4 November 1948–31 December 1949 for an exchange of goods to the value of $10 million on each side.

With Roumania agreement concluded on 22 June 1948 for turnover to the value of £5 million a year. Hungary to supply light industrial goods, electrical materials, precision tools, agricultural machinery, materials for railways against oil, oil products, timber, chemicals, certain metals, soda, bituminous materials, lead, salt.

POLAND

With Albania 22 January 1949. Total value $4 million. Rolling stock, coastal vessels, metal goods, machine tools, and electric equipment against copper pyrites, cotton, oil and tobacco.

With Bulgaria, Czechoslovakia, Hungary (see above).

With Roumania economic co-operation and trade agreement concluded on 10 September 1948 for a period of five years. Machinery, technical instruments, various raw materials against oil and mining products. Trade agreement of 16 December 1948 to the value of $5 million. Coke, foundry products, machinery, industrial equipment, and textiles against petroleum products, timber, meat, fats, foodstuffs.

ROUMANIA

With Albania 2 April 1949.

With Bulgaria, Czechoslovakia, Hungary, Poland (see above).

SOVIET ZONE OF GERMANY

With Bulgaria 26 August 1948 to the value of $6 million.

With Czechoslovakia 21 July 1948 to the value of $18·5 million.

With Finland 29 September 1948.

With Hungary 30 June 1948.

With Poland 29 March 1949 to the value of $152 million during 1949, and of 8 June 1949 for the delivery by Germany of machinery and industrial equipment to the value of $30 million during 1949–50.

With Yugoslavia, a trade agreement was concluded in April 1947 but it is presumably no longer in force.

YUGOSLAVIA[1]

With Bulgaria agreements of March and August 1947 for delivery of chemicals for the tanning industry, sulphuric acid, medicines, against tobacco, cotton, seeds, machines for processing cotton.

With Czechoslovakia. Agreement signed 1 March 1949 to be valid until 30 December 1950 for delivery of Yugoslav fodder, oil seeds, meat, poultry, timber, leather, hemp, iron, chromium ores, non-ferrous metals, tobacco, wine and other agricultural produce, against Czechoslovak industrial equipment, motor cars, spare parts, chemicals, glass, tyres, electro-technical materials, consumer goods. (In 1948 Yugoslavia supplied 20 per cent of Czechoslovakia's requirements of copper, 50 per cent of lead, 60 per cent of pyrites.)

With Hungary. Trade agreement concluded in December 1946, later extended; a fifteen years' agreement signed in May 1947 for the erection of two aluminium plants in Yugoslavia; a five years' investment agreement concluded in June 1947 for the construction of power stations and industrial plant in Yugoslavia. Hungary received from Yugoslavia 30 per cent of its requirements of iron ore and caustic soda, 50 per cent of ammonia carbonate, 100 per cent of copper, lead, pyrites. Hungary's deliveries included machinery, electro-machinery, locomotives, rolling stock, machine tools. In 1947 Hungary was already behind with her deliveries by $2·89 million, and in 1948 by another $1·16 million.

With Poland. Trade agreement of May and economic agreement of November 1947, both for five years. For delivery of Yugoslav non-ferrous metals, and wheat against coke, electro-products, steel. The trade agreement of January 1949 foresaw only 25 per cent of the 1948 trade.

With Roumania. Agreement of 5 February 1948 for the delivery of finished products from coke and cast iron sent by Yugoslavia.

[1] Owing to the Cominform conflict all trade agreements with Yugoslavia were either denounced or suspended in the summer of 1949.

7. EXCHANGE RATES IN RELATION TO U.S. DOLLAR*

	1938	1945	1946	1947	1948	1949
BULGARIA						
leva	84·37	—	288	288	288	288
CZECHOSLOVAKIA						
korunas	28·88	50·15	50·15	50·15	50·15	50·15
HUNGARY						
forints	3·401 pengös	—	11·827	11·827	11·827	11·827
POLAND						
zlotys						
Official rate ⎱	5·30	—	102	102	102	102
Premium ⎰					402†	402
ROUMANIA						
lei	101·54		not			
	140·12	3·653	given	153	153	153
	(with prem.)					
YUGOSLAVIA						
dinars	43·43	50·06	50·00	50·00	—	—

* With Eastern European countries, as quoted by the International Monetary Fund, Washington, in *International Financial Statistics*, December 1949. (These figures are given as selling rates, except in the case of Yugoslavia, where the smount is quoted as 'official exchange rate'.)

† Since its establishment in 1946 the current official rate of 100 zl. per U.S. dollar has applied to certain types of remittances only. Foreign trade being largely conducted by State organizations, a premium surcharge of 300 zl. per U.S. dollar, effective January 1948, is paid or charged on practically all financial transfers abroad, making the effective rate for such transactions 400 zl. per U.S. dollar.

8. EXCHANGE RATES IN RELATION TO THE ROUBLE
[*New York Times* (4 January 1950)]

	rouble value
Albanian leki (per 100)	10·60
English pound sterling	14·84
Bulgarian leva (per 100)	1·86
Hungarian forint (per 100)	45·49
Polish zloty (per 1,000)	13·25
Roumanian lei (per 1,000)	35·33
United States dollar	5·30
Czechoslovak crown (per 100)	10·50
Yugoslav dinar	—

9. AGREEMENTS BETWEEN USSR AND EASTERN EUROPE
(excluding armistice and peace agreements)

	Date	Page
CZECHOSLOVAKIA		
Mutual aid	July 1941	12
Friendship, mutual assistance and post-war collaboration	Dec. 1943	12
Military and monetary matters	May, July 1944	12
Trade	24 Sept. 1945	19–20
Trade	12 Apr. 1946	20–2
Railways	Dec. 1946	23
Trade (five-year treaty)	11 Dec. 1947	25–9
Trade and Navigation	11 Dec. 1947	26
Loan	11 Dec. 1947	26
Scientific and technical co-operation	11 Dec. 1947	27
Protocol for 1949 deliveries	Oct. 1948	29–31
Delivery of Soviet capital goods	July 1949	31–2
POLAND		
Friendship, mutual assistance and post-war collaboration	21 Apr. 1945	39
Frontier and reparations (from Germany)	16 Aug. 1945	39–40
Trade	July 1945	40
Trade	12 Apr. 1946	40–1
Economic and military aid	5 Mar. 1947	41
Scientific and technical co-operation	5 Mar. 1947	41
Financial matters, supply of arms, granting of gold credit, etc.	May 1947	41
Trade	Aug. 1947	42
Grain deliveries from USSR	Aug.-Sept. 1947	42
Trade (five-year treaty)	26 Jan. 1948	42–3
Soviet industrial equipment and loan	26 Jan. 1948	43
Trade	May 1948	44–5
Protocol for 1949 deliveries	15 Jan. 1949	45
BULGARIA		
Economic agreement	14 Mar. 1945	51
Trade	27 Apr. 1946	52
Trade	5 July 1947	53
Soviet industrial equipment on credit	23 Aug. 1947	53
Friendship, co-operation and mutual assistance (twenty years)	18 Mar. 1948	53
Trade and Navigation	1 Apr. 1948	53
Trade	1 Apr. 1948	54
Protocol for 1949 deliveries	18 Jan. 1949	54

	Date	Page
HUNGARY		
Joint companies	Mar.-Apr. 1945	65
Trade	Aug. 1945	63–4
Economic agreement (five years)	Dec. 1945	62–3
Trade and Navigation	15 July 1947	68–9
Reduction of reparation payments	24 July 1947	69
German assets, Soviet and joint companies, etc.	9 Dec. 1947	70–1
Friendship, co-operation and mutual assistance (twenty years)	18 Feb. 1948	71
Trade	2 Oct. 1948	71–2
Machinery for USSR	2 Oct. 1948	72
ROUMANIA		
Economic and trade agreement	8 May 1945	79–80
Agreement on economic and political matters, including reduction of reparation payments	12 Sept. 1945	81
Trade and Navigation	20 Feb. 1947	81–2
Trade	20 Feb. 1947	82
Railways	12 June 1947	82–3
Friendship, co-operation and mutual assistance (twenty years)	4 Feb. 1948	83
Trade	18 Feb. 1948	83
Trade	24 Jan. 1949	84
Technical assistance	24 Jan. 1949	84
YUGOSLAVIA (all agreements denounced or suspended)		
Friendship, co-operation and mutual assistance (twenty years)	13 Apr. 1945	89
Trade	13 Apr. 1945	89
Trade	8 June 1946	89
Trade and payments	5 July 1947	91
Soviet industrial equipment on credit, and technical assistance	25 July 1947	91
Protocol for 1949 deliveries	27 Dec. 1948	92–3

INDEX

(Supplementary to Table of Contents)

CENTRAL AND SOUTH EAST EUROPE, 1945–1948

Edited by R. R. BETTS

The purpose of this study is to provide a handy record of those political and economic events in Central and South East Europe which, since its liberation from the Germans, have transformed society and government there. The story of events during the three fateful years 1945–8 has been recounted for each country in turn, in the order of their liberation: that is, starting with Roumania, and proceeding by way of Bulgaria, Yugoslavia, Hungary, and Poland to Czechoslovakia, which was the last to be freed.

The authors of the various chapters are as follows: E. D. Tappe, Lecturer in Roumanian at the School of Slavonic and East European Studies, University of London (ROUMANIA); Phyllis Auty, Lecturer in the History of South Eastern Europe in the same School (BULGARIA and YUGOSLAVIA); Elizabeth Wiskemann (HUNGARY); Brian Ireland (POLAND); and Professor R. R. Betts, Masaryk Professor of Central European History in the University of London (CZECHOSLOVAKIA and concluding chapter).

Price 18s. *net*

SOVIET TRADE UNIONS
Their Place in Soviet Labour Policy

By ISAAC DEUTSCHER

Author of *Stalin: A Political Biography*

Mr Deutscher's book traces the road followed by the Soviet trade unions from 1917, when they were independent organizations of the Russian working class, to their present status as more or less compulsory State agencies, used to further the Government's economic policies and to administer the system of social insurance through the vast Trade Union network. It is the first comprehensive historical account of the Soviet trade unions to be published in English.

Price 7s. 6d. *net*

ROYAL INSTITUTE OF INTERNATIONAL AFFAIRS

London: Chatham House, 10 St James's Square, S.W.1
New York: 542 Fifth Avenue, New York 19, N.Y.